Williams College

Williams College

AN ARCHITECTURAL TOUR BY

Eugene J. Johnson and

Michael J. Lewis

PHOTOGRAPHY BY RALPH LIEBERMAN

FOREWORD BY ADAM FALK

PRINCETON ARCHITECTURAL PRESS
NEW YORK

For **Sheafe Satterthwaite**,

colleague and dear friend,

who teaches us that everything is interesting,

if you ask the right questions

PUBLISHED BY
Princeton Architectural Press
A McEvoy Group company
202 Warren Street, Hudson, NY 12534
www.papress.com

Princeton Architectural Press is a leading publisher in architecture, design, photography, landscape, and visual culture. We create fine books and stationery of unsurpassed quality and production values. With more than one thousand titles published, we find design everywhere and in the most unlikely places.

SERIES EDITOR: Jan Cigliano Hartman
EDITOR: Linda Lee
LAYOUT: Adrianna Sutton
MAPMAKER: John Wang

Frontispiece: Mission Park Dormitory

SPECIAL THANKS TO: Janet Behning, Abby Bussel, Benjamin English, Susan Hershberg, Kristen Hewitt, Lia Hunt, Valerie Kamen, Jennifer Lippert, Sara McKay, Parker Menzimer, Eliana Miller, Nina Pick, Wes Seeley, Rob Shaeffer, Sara Stemen, Marisa Tesoro, Paul Wagner, and Joseph Weston of Princeton Architectural Press
—Kevin C. Lippert, publisher

LIBRARY OF CONGRESS CATALOGING-IN-PUBLICATION DATA
Names: Johnson, Eugene J., 1937– author. | Lewis, Michael J., 1957– author.
Title: Williams College: the campus guide: an architectural tour / by
  Eugene J. Johnson and Michael J. Lewis; photography by Ralph Lieberman;
  foreword by Adam Falk.
Description: First edition. | New York: Princeton Architectural Press, [2018]
  | Series: Campus guides | Includes bibliographical references and index.
Identifiers: LCCN 2018022154 | ISBN 9781616897116 (paperback: alk. paper)
Subjects: LCSH: Williams College—Buildings. | Williams College—History.
Classification: LCC LD6073 .J64 2018 | DDC 378.744/1—dc23
LC record available at https://lccn.loc.gov/2018022154

Contents

An architectural guidebook should be lightweight, but only in the physical sense. It walks a perilous line between scholarship and portability, the line where breeziness turns into inconsequence. Scholarly books on architecture do not travel well. They typically lie open on desks or library tables, benign unless dropped on a foot. We have opted for a compromise. We treat the most important buildings on campus with the seriousness they are due, while lesser structures are treated with briefer statements (or none at all) that reflect their lesser artistic or historical value. We hope that the longer entries will be read on on site, but we realize that some users may choose to read them in the comfort of a lounge chair before or after a direct visit, or maybe even both. The context for all the college buildings, by now built over more than 225 years, is laid out in the introduction, organized chronologically by the succession of presidents. Some, like Harry A. Garfield or John E. Sawyer, were keenly interested in architecture; others, like Mark Hopkins, were not. And yet each had a profound impact on the architecture of the campus. The visitor may want to have a look at the introduction before setting out on foot.

The Princeton Architectural Press series on American campuses, to which this volume belongs, has a specific format based on walks. These walks include buildings that are close to one another and can easily be visited on foot. This convenience for the traveler produces some strange neighbors on the page, so history takes a backseat to propinquity. This guide is arranged in six Walks, beginning at the center of the campus with the first building of the institution, West College (1790). Subsequent Walks revolve around West and end, on Walk Six, at the Sterling and Francine Clark Art Institute, a separate entity but so closely connected to the college that it had to be included. Appended is an excursion to outlying properties.

Unusually for a guidebook, we have included quite a lot of historical material. This is not just a book about how the campus looks at this particular moment; it is also an account of how some buildings and locales have changed over time. We believe that the experience of the buildings as they appear now can be greatly enhanced by making clear how the buildings once looked or what preceded them on the same site.

We learned a lot while writing the book: the crucial role of Congregationalism in the early decades; the gradual replacement of theology by science as a central part of the curriculum; the persistence of the problems that fraternities caused in the social life of the campus and the leadership they took in building up-to-date architecture; conversely, the failure of the college to find a totally satisfactory substitute for fraternities, save for the fact that their demise led to some of the best architecture Williams has ever built. We hope that users of this book, particularly those who have known and loved Williams for a long time, will find that after wandering the campus with this guide in hand, they have also come to an enriched understanding of this place, semi-isolated in its mountain fastness.

Foreword

When I heard that E. J. Johnson and Michael Lewis were writing a guide to the architecture of Williams College, my first thought was: who better to undertake such a quixotic task?

As anyone who has visited the campus knows, there is no single Williams architectural style. Instead, we embody a central precept of academic architecture: colleges and universities build to suit the ways we teach and live. As those ways evolve—often in keeping with societal notions of what higher learning should be—so do our buildings. From the classical, inward orientation of Griffin to the walls of glass that make learning visible in the new Sawyer Library, each Williams building in some way captures the thinking of its time.

E. J. and Michael are among the very few people we could trust to guide us through this ever-shifting landscape. They were also especially fortunate to partner with Ralph Lieberman, the distinguished architectural historian and photographer, and a longtime collaborator with both, who produced the exquisite photography for this book. The resulting work is historically insightful, compulsively readable, visually stunning, and infused with a healthy dose of irreverence. After all, not all architectural ideas are as effective in practice as they seemed to be on paper. The authors have their opinions about which of our buildings are more or less successful—as will every reader of this book. We won't all agree on the answers. But, being the great Williams teachers they are, Mike and E. J. make the debate one worth having. And entertaining, too.

You don't need to be steeped in architectural theory to grasp the effect of Williams's architectural diversity. All that's required is a stroll across campus; for example, along the quad past old Hopkins, new Schapiro and Hollander, toward a renovated Chapin. Or along Main Street, with West College and the new Science Center on one side and the '62 Center for Theatre and Dance on the other. Or up beyond Dodd toward Poker Flats. Or any one of the many other possible routes along which established edifices stand cheek by jowl with more recent arrivals. Nor can we overlook the lawns, meadows, and forests that are so important to the character of this place. In fact, at Williams we increasingly think of our campus in environmental, as well as intellectual and developmental, terms. That shift, too, is embodied in our approach to building, which now incorporates numerous green practices.

Colleges are also richly human environments, shaped by the way we live in and even remember them. Alumni opinions about campus buildings are often rooted in personal experience and memory, as much or more than they are in aesthetic or pedagogical principles. You may fondly remember visiting a favorite teacher in a cramped office in Clark. Or a special evening with friends in the fortress-like Mission Park. Structure, use, memory: in reality we're dealing with not one Williams College but thousands, each mapped in someone's mind and heart, all laid atop a single, physical location.

What a wonderful, living thing a campus is. Fortunately, E. J. Johnson and Michael Lewis are brave and foolhardy enough to take on the task of describing this complex space we call Williams. Their work is a singular history of the college: not just of its structures, but of us as the people who built and occupied and shaped them, while they in turn shaped us.

E. J. and Michael's book has already deepened my appreciation and love for Williams. I hope it will do the same for you.

Adam Falk
President, 2010–17

Ruben Belding	33	34	John Moffat
Micah Harrington	31	32	Elisha Williams junr
Mr Nathl Russel	29	30	Thomas Train
George Williams Esqr	27	28	Isaac Wyman
Samuel Avery	25	26	Josiah Dean
Thomas Moffat	23	24	William Chedester
Jehiel Dickinson	21	22	Benja Simons
John Chamberlain	19	20	Eneas Mackey
Moses Graves	17	18	Joel Dickinson
Thomas Moffit	15	16	Josiah Williams
Ezekiel Foster	13	14	Abner Robards
Joseph Smith	11	12	Saml Wills
Seth Hutson	9	10	Ezekiel ...
John Shepherd Esq (Jacob Williams)		8	Ezk ... junr
Saml Calhoon	5	6	Wm Chedester
Mr Simn Woodbridge	3	4	Col Partridge
Saml Brown Junr	1	2	Lt Joseph Wyman

School	35	36	Ministers
Saml Calhoon	37	38	Ministry
Lt Saml Brown	39	40	Elisha Hawley
Lt Elisha Chapin	41	42	John Bush
Elijah Brown	43	44	Josiah Stevens
Obadiah Dickinson	45	46	John Moffit
Joseph Hawley Esqr	47	48	Lt Moses Graves
Daniel Hause	49	50	Saml Taylor
Ens Elisha Allis	51	52	Saml Smith
Col ...	53	54	Lt Saml Brown
Oliver Avery	55	56	Ebenezer Graves
		58	Lt Saml Brown
		59	John Crafford
		60	Aaron Denio
		61	Obadiah Dickinson
		62	Eneas McKey
		63	Daniel Donielson

Brook

at large

West 26 o 15 o

Nath... 7 Harvey

The story of Williams College is one of the more unlikely in the annals of American higher education. Founded in 1793 in the remotest inland corner of Massachusetts to educate local youth for the ministry, by the early twenty-first century it had become an institution repeatedly selected as the leading liberal arts college in the United States in the annual *U.S. News and World Report* survey of American universities and colleges. In its own way, the architecture of the college tells that remarkable tale.[1]

When Captain Ephraim Williams, founder of Williams College, took command in 1745 of Fort Massachusetts in the mountainous wilderness of the northwest corner of the colony, he found himself in the middle of a conflict between two great European powers. As the French settled in Canada and the English moved west from Massachusetts Bay, they competed over that remote spot. Fort Massachusetts, erected on the banks of the Hoosac River in what is now North Adams, was intended to project English power in a region the British claimed. The geography made the area vulnerable to French raiding parties and their indigenous allies, who could come down from Canada via Lake Champlain to despoil settlements in the Hudson Valley and western Massachusetts. The Hoosac Valley, its river a tributary of the Hudson, offered passage through the Taconic Mountains for raids on English settlers. In 1746 Williams was fortunate enough to be away from Fort Massachusetts when it was seized and burned by a force of seven hundred to nine hundred French people and natives, who marched the surrendered garrison to Canada as prisoners. Many died.[2]

The fort was quickly rebuilt, Williams resumed his command, and in 1750 he ordered a survey of the area. Two towns were laid out, West Hoosac and East Hoosac, destined to become Williamstown and Adams, respectively. In West Hoosac, Williams established sixty-three lots of ten to twelve acres each, recorded in a plan that is still preserved. Williams himself bought lots 8 and 10, well watered by Hemlock Brook; fifteen soldiers under his command purchased lots as well. Owners of the new lots were required to build within two years a house eighteen by fifteen feet, with an interior height of no less than seven feet. The area being heavily forested, owners were required to clear and fence five acres for agricultural purposes.

In this settlement a new bastion, Fort West Hoosac, was erected to protect the inhabitants and project the power of the English even farther west. The protection was needed. On July 11, 1756, three men, out looking for their cows,

The original plan of Williamstown, commissioned in 1750 by Captain Ephraim Williams. He needed a settlement for the soldiers under his command at nearby Fort Massachusetts, which stood on the Hoosac River in present-day North Adams, and his chief concern was to lay out equally sized building lots. This explains the plan's oddest feature: while it notes the streams that flow through the site, it completely ignores the dramatically undulating topography.

were scalped near the banks of Hemlock Brook by a raiding party from Canada. Settling this new town had been premature, at least in terms of safety. French raids from Canada did not cease until 1760, when the English successfully drove the French from that territory.

Williams's plan of 1750 for West Hoosac centered on a wide east–west thoroughfare, Main Street, that intersected two cross streets named North and South. The right-angled intersection of North and South Streets was intended to be the town center, with lots for a minister's house and a school specified on the corners. Williams's simple conceptual plan does not show the layout of the intersection as it actually came to be; west of the intersection a rectangular area of grass and trees, now known as Field Park, divided Main Street into two parts that eventually rejoined to continue west. West Hoosac was incorporated as Williamstown in 1765. Three years later the first meetinghouse, an essential component of any new New England town, rose on that grassy plot that became the town green.

In 1755 Williams, now a colonel, passed through Albany, New York, on his way to fight the French at Lake George. There he wrote a will that specified that the residue of his estate be used to found a free school in West Hoosac, provided that the town be located in Massachusetts (the border with New York was not clearly defined until 1787) and renamed Williamstown. Should any money be left over, another free school might be founded in Adams, the adjoining town to the east. The executors of his estate were charged with seeing his wishes carried out. In September 1755 Williams was killed in an ambush at the Battle of Lake George, setting in motion the events that led to the renaming of the town and the founding of an institution to educate the offspring of those who had purchased lots there. His interest lay in the futures of the families of the men who had been under his command, and in the perpetuation of his name.

Williams is an enigmatic figure. Born in 1714 in Newton, Massachusetts, he lost his mother at an early age and was largely raised by his maternal grandfather. He went to sea rather than to college, so that he had some experience of Europe but none of higher education. He barely appears in historical records before his appointment in 1745 as commander of Fort Massachusetts—a position he surely owed to the considerable political influence of the extended Williams family in the western part of the colony. There is no evidence that he had previous military experience. He never settled down in one place, and he did not marry and start a family. When he wrote his will, he called Hatfield, in Hampshire County just north of Northampton, his residence, but he also owned property in Stockbridge, Massachusetts, that he had purchased from his father, Ephraim Sr., who had moved there with a second wife and a second crop of children in 1739, only a month after the town was incorporated. In his will Williams Jr. provided for a plethora of relatives: brother and sister, half brothers and half sisters, stepmother, and numerous cousins. Clearly, this extended family was of great importance to him, perhaps because he had been raised largely apart from it. Had he married and sired children, his will would have been quite different, and there would be no Williams College. His soldiers and their offspring, in effect, became his progeny. Although his own education does not seem to have been extensive, he was devoted to the idea of education.

No one rushed to carry out Williams's wishes. Thirty years later, in 1785, the General Court of Massachusetts finally created "The Trustees of the Donation of Ephraim Williams, Esq., for maintaining a Free School in Williamstown." By then, the remains of the estate came to $9,157, a sum the trustees deemed insufficient to erect a structure to house the school; there was no extra cash for a second free school in Adams. The trustees petitioned the state to allow a lottery to raise the needed funds; enough money was gathered, largely from locals. In 1790 the Free School opened in its new building, now known as West College.

The plan of 1750 took no note of the hilly topography on which the lots were laid out. Like a roller coaster, Main Street rises four times from east to west to "eminences" and then slopes into low points. The trustees chose for the site of the school the second eminence from the east, a commanding point. There they

The view of Main Street looking west from Griffin Hall shows the first college building, West College, in the center. To its right is the Meeting House that once faced Main Street from its commanding location at the eastern edge of the town green, now known as Field Park.

raised West College, athwart the broad right-of-way of the town-owned Main Street, a four-story, rectangular, brick structure with a cupola, the largest building by far in the rural, agricultural settlement. From this eminence the educational institution foreseen by Williams commanded the town.

Within three years the ambition of the trustees of the Free School had grown to the point that they chose to ignore the terms of Ephraim Williams's will. Unlike the founder, the majority of the nine trustees were college graduates, five from Yale and one from Princeton. They petitioned the General Court of Massachusetts to allow them to create a college, an institution of higher learning that would draw students from distant points and no longer focus principally on the free education of local youth that Williams had specified. The petitioners, however, stressed the need for an affordable education for young men of the town unable to afford travel to distant schools. At that time the only colleges in New England were Harvard, Yale, and Dartmouth. In a hardly subtle reference to the only other institution of higher education in the Commonwealth, Harvard, they noted that "Williamstown, being an inland place, will not be exposed to those temptations and allurements, which are peculiarly incident to Seaport towns."[3]

The difference in intent between the Free School and the college is made painfully clear by the change in requirements for entry. Students wishing to matriculate at the Free School had only to demonstrate that they could read English well. Those seeking entrance to the college had to "accurately read, parse, and construe to the satisfaction of the President and Tutor Virgil's *Aeneid*, Tully's [Cicero's] Orations and the Evangelists in Greek."[4] The requirement in Greek, however, could be substituted by a knowledge of French, to attract students from Quebec. In 1793 Williams College replaced the Williamstown Free School.

In its first years the college flourished, and soon, in 1798, a second multipurpose structure, East College, rose up to accommodate the growing enrollments. At about the same time, two additional large and important town structures arose: a new meetinghouse on the green, and a tavern, later known as the Mansion House, on the northeast corner of the intersection of Main and North Streets. For the first time, Williamstown began to have a sense of spatial organization, visible in a panoramic view made around 1840 that shows West College on its eminence toward the left side and East College toward the right, occupying a second eminence. The placing of East College on that height foreordained that the center of the town, growing more and more focused on the college, would shift away from the intersection of North, South, and Main, even though that crossroads boasted the Meeting House and the tavern, two buildings crucial to the town's life.

Particularly satisfying artistically is a slightly earlier lithograph of circa 1830 by James Kidder that shows a cropped version of the engraving of circa 1840. The two original college buildings, West and East, established an aesthetic principle often followed in Williams College structures: sharp-edged, planar, geometric solids inserted into a curvaceous landscape against the backdrop of forests and

A part of the easterly view of WILLIAMSTOWN *seen from the fourth story Old College.*

Looking east from West College toward the newly constructed East College perched on the first "eminence" that greeted visitors coming into town from the east. A purely utilitarian brick rectangle, with four stories and four chimneys, East loomed over the domestic structures that characterized the rest of the village: town and gown in an early manifestation.

This print can be dated to just before 1841, because it shows at the far right the dome on the Hopkins Observatory that blew off in January of that year in a windstorm. The dome was replaced by a cylinder. (See Walk Three, p. 132.)

The lithograph by James Kidder, made around 1830, shows bucolic Williamstown, during the presidency of Edward Dorr Griffin, whose pedimented New Chapel (now Griffin Hall) turns its long side to Main Street. The once-forested site has been cleared. The open fields are fenced to contain the livestock that roamed the village. A very picturesque cow lolls where one day cars would crowd Spring Street.

mountains, with breathing space among the buildings that allows the forms of nature to frame and soften the hard-edged efforts of humans. The native forests were cleared away, replaced by fences to control the livestock that roamed the open spaces. Note the cow resting in the lithograph where Spring Street eventually would appear. In the early nineteenth century the economy of Williamstown largely depended on agriculture.

The third building that figures prominently in the Kidder lithograph is the New Chapel, now Griffin Hall, opened in 1828 across Main Street from East College. The third major institutional structure, the New Chapel was the first to have its long axis parallel to the street. Griffin Hall is the ultimately happy outcome of the most perilous moment in the college's history. Although Yale College was the source for the plans for East and possibly for West, Yale was not the source for the disposition of buildings in the landscape. At Yale, the early buildings of the eighteenth century were lined up side by side in a row to face the New Haven Green. This disposition of structures creating a visual wall had a number of progeny in later academic plans, such as that for Amherst College. But Williams College struck off in its own direction, to respond to the hilly topography by occupying high points along the axis of Main Street.

While Williams College had prospered in its early years, as the need to erect East College attests, by the middle of the second decade of the nineteenth century enrollment was faltering, and the economic stability of the institution was in question. Newly established Union College in New York and Middlebury in

George Warner's photograph of Griffin Hall, taken in the 1860s, shows the steep slope of Main Street, once known as Consumption Hill, which slowed the passage of the visitor from the east. This gave time to admire one of the most sophisticated architectural achievements of this corner of the Commonwealth of Massachusetts. The one-story wing to the right housed the chemistry classroom, awkwardly attached to the east face of the building in the 1840s.

Vermont were attracting students from Williams. In 1815, when the first president, Ebenezer Fitch, resigned because of failing health, a majority of the trustees began to contemplate moving Williams to the Connecticut River valley to escape the remote locale of Williamstown. Fitch had not been a charismatic leader, particularly in his later presidential years. The new president, Zephaniah Swift Moore, may have accepted that position with the understanding that he would supervise a move over the mountains to a more easily accessible site in Hampshire County. In 1818 the newly established Amherst Academy petitioned the Williams College trustees to link the two institutions and to establish the college there. The trustees demurred but appointed three disinterested agents from three other states to seek out a site in Hampshire County. They chose Northampton.

By the next year such enthusiasm for the move had developed in that town and its environs that pledges for $35,003.33 were raised to support the move. The Williams trustees, however, estimated that $50,000 would be needed. Widespread opposition arose in the Berkshires, where hundreds of people joined in a subscription to keep the college in place. Touchingly, the sums pledged ranged from $2.50 to $800, and added up to roughly $18,000. Despite the local opposition, in 1820 the Williams trustees petitioned the legislature for permission to "remove Williams College to Northampton," which was finally denied in 1825. Even before the legislature acted on the trustees' petition to move the college, Moore accepted an invitation to become head of Amherst Academy and announced his intended resignation after Commencement Day, August 25, 1821. Fifteen students followed him over the mountains to Amherst, but they were less than half of the forty students who abandoned the college for other institutions at this calamitous moment. The forty or so students who remained, however, were determined to keep the institution going. On that Commencement Day of Moore's resignation, the college's supporters founded the first Society of Alumni in the United States. Williams College was not going to fail without a struggle.

Also at the same commencement of 1821 a new college president, Edward Dorr Griffin, appeared on the platform. A graduate of Yale, Griffin for two years had held the chair of Pulpit Eloquence at the recently founded Andover Theological Seminary. His skill as a preacher attracted students to Williams, and the college began to get back on its feet economically.

The citizens of Williamstown in 1820 had already rallied to provide financial support to the college by raising a hefty subscription. At their September meeting in 1825 the trustees, eager to create visible signs of the college's renewed vitality, decided to build a new chapel and create a new professorship. In 1826 Griffin, who pledged $1,000 of his own funds, through superhuman efforts raised $25,000 in three months—$15,000 for the professorship and $10,000 for the building. Griffin, who credited a series of popular religious revivals among students and townsfolk with helping him raise the money, appears to have been the designer of the new chapel, a bold statement about the college's future. By placing the building on the eastern eminence, Griffin emphatically claimed the land between East and West Colleges as the center of the campus, an area that one day would also become the town's center. These three brick buildings in the landscape, visible in the Kidder lithograph of circa 1830, were the physical manifestation of the college when its first great president, Mark Hopkins (Class of 1824), was inaugurated as the fourth head of the institution in 1836.

* * *

The ideal college is Mark Hopkins on one end of a log and a student on the other.
—attributed to James A. Garfield

It is curious that the best-known epigram about Hopkins concerns his teaching and not his presidency, the longest in college history. But every student who attended Williams between 1836 and 1872 knew him as a presence in the classroom. His courses were required, as were all courses in those days, and he left his mark on the college in a way that is no longer conceivable today. He is the classic example of that long-vanished species, the teaching administrator.

If you believe that a college is nothing more than an elaborated log, then you will not worry too much about its buildings and physical plant. And this was the case with Hopkins, a college president who was indifferent to

View of Williams
College, after 1847

fundraising—another vanished species—and did not think in terms of expansion and development. In fact, he assumed the presidency on the explicit condition that he not be obliged to solicit funds. He was even slow to spot a gift when it was dangled in front of him. The story told in Frederick Rudolph's *Mark Hopkins and the Log* (1956) is remarkable: early in 1846, Hopkins was riding in a carriage in Boston with Amos Lawrence, the textile magnate and philanthropist, who asked if there was any way he could be helpful to the college. After brief consideration, Hopkins replied that he "could not think of a thing"—an act that today would be regarded as criminal negligence. Only after sleeping on it did Hopkins recall that the college desperately needed a library building. He came to his senses the next morning and remembered that the trustees had authorized the building of a modest library. Lawrence promptly agreed to pay for it, and construction began the following May.

The pattern held true during the rest of Hopkins's presidency. When compelled to build, as he was when East College burned to the ground, he typically built plain, utilitarian structures. This was in part due to his lingering Calvinist suspicion of pomp, but it was also because of the brutal fact of the college's poverty. Kellogg Hall (1847), which stood near the site of Jesup Hall, shows his characteristic frugality. Prim and unlovely, without a single inch of decorative carving, the building crowded two stories of dormitories above its classrooms. This was not unusual: almost everything Hopkins built suffered from the same mixing of functions that characterized West College itself, which simultaneously served as classroom, library, chapel, and dormitory. The idea that a building should be devoted to a single purpose, which should decisively determine its form and style, came late to Williams. Lawrence Hall (1846) was a lonely exception to this pattern in these early years.

Another building that suffered from trying to do too much with too little was the original Goodrich Hall (1864), which stood near where Thompson

This undated photograph is all that remains of Kellogg Hall (1847), a combination classroom-dormitory building with one innovative feature: permanent benches mounted on the walls of its classrooms. Previously, the seats in West Hall's recitation rooms were owned by the freshmen and sophomores—who sold them in turn to the members of the next class!

Memorial Chapel now rises. Once again, the donor's gift practically fell into Hopkins's lap. His sister Mary was the wife of John Z. Goodrich, a businessman in nearby Stockbridge and a major figure in the founding of the Republican Party. Mary was evidently the family philanthropist, and in 1863 she pushed her husband to fund both a public library in Stockbridge and a "fine capacious stone edifice" for Williams College.[5] Once again, Hopkins tried to cram as many uses into the building as possible: a bowling alley in the basement, chemistry laboratories on the first floor, and a gymnasium above. There cannot have been many of those. Goodrich selected the architect John F. Edwards of Boston, who wrapped the bewildering program in an Early Gothic cocoon, presumably to match the college chapel across the street. (This first Goodrich Hall was demolished to make room for Thompson Memorial Chapel, but its name survived, transferred to the first freestanding college chapel building, today known as Goodrich.) Charles Yeomans's hand-colored lithograph shows the campus at the end of the first decade of the Hopkins presidency.

This detail of a lithograph by Charles Yeomans, Class of 1856, shows with great accuracy the center of the campus in the view from Stone Hill. In the middle is the dominant mass of Griffin Hall, its cupola then the highest point of the college. Just to the right of it is the octagon of Lawrence Hall, seen better here than in any other early view of the college. The new Spring Street, its top end already lined with buildings on both sides, runs down the little valley west of Griffin and Lawrence.

On October 1, 1863, the *Berkshire Eagle* announced that an anonymous donor was giving Williams a "large stone building...partly for gymnastic and partly for literary purposes." That discreet donor was none other than the owner of the *Berkshire Eagle* himself, John Z. Goodrich. This first Goodrich Hall stood until 1902.

CHAPTER LODGE (Λ) OF THE DELTA-PSI FRATERNITY. WILLIAMS COLLEGE.

TOP LEFT The old and the new: after half a century of building plain brick parallelograms, Williams College embraced the bewildering variety of Victorian architecture. This photograph from the 1860s shows, from left to right, the white-painted boxes of East and South College (1842), the eclectic Greek-*Rundbogenstil* confection of Lawrence Hall (1847), and the rusticated stone prism of the picturesque Gothic chapel (1859). Buildings would now vary wildly in material, shape, and style, something that was felt at the time to be a great liberation. After another half century passed, the Victorian era would be scorned as a disorderly and confused interlude.

BOTTOM LEFT College Hall (1872), with its twenty-two rooms, served as a boardinghouse for the college's less prosperous students, who gave it its nickname, "Hash House." It was built and perhaps designed by Harry B. Curtis, a prominent Williamstown builder. It was demolished to make way for Stetson Library.

TOP RIGHT When Nathan Jackson discovered that it cost $3,500 to build Jackson Hall, a thousand more than he had donated, he promptly sent the college a check in that amount "because he could not consent to have others at any expense for a building which bears his name."

BOTTOM RIGHT Had William T. Hallett built his fraternity house for Delta Psi, it would have been among America's boldest essays in the High Victorian Gothic. But in architecture, as in much of life, timing is everything: 1860 was a bad year to propose a new building. His hopeful design was shelved and forgotten, but not before he sent this photograph of his drawing to the Royal Institute of British Architects.

If the college's architecture was conservative, so was its classical curriculum, which remained oriented toward the grooming of Congregationalist ministers. The modern sciences, which were still grouped under the rubric of natural history, only slowly affected the curriculum. The first tangible sign that science would play a conspicuous role at the college came in 1855, with Jackson Hall, a strikingly innovative building for its day, with a skylit gallery for specimens and a lecture room in an adjoining tower. But Hopkins had virtually nothing to do with Jackson Hall. The impulse came from the student-run Lyceum of Natural History, and it was these students who recruited the donor, Nathan Jackson, of New York, a distant relative of Ephraim Williams.

Otherwise, Hopkins remained resistant to innovation, as when he dismissed the suggestion of Arthur Latham Perry, the professor of economics, that he reserve part of Mission Park for use as the college cemetery. In this instance, thankfully, he was overruled. In general, the college's students were more restless and curious about architecture than its trustees. By far the most radical building proposed during Hopkins's tenure was the fraternity house of Delta Psi (1860). This was a daring essay in High Victorian pyrotechnics, slashed with vivid bands of color that evoked layers of geological strata, just as John Ruskin recommended. Clearly, Williams students had read his *Stones of Venice*— and just as clearly, their professors had not.

There is something endearing about Hopkins's indifference to the vagaries of changing fashion, which is of a piece with his teaching. Instead of compelling memorized recitations, he preferred the open-ended Socratic method. He was famous for his "pill box," a tin box in which the names of all the students were recorded on cardboard slips, which he would select at random. The student whose name was called would have to instantly stand and be asked a question, not to recall a passage from memory but to take a position and defend it. J. H. Denison, Hopkins's first biographer, said his method was not "to pump philosophy into men but to draw it out from them." Such a president, it is easy to see, could indeed have done this sitting on a log. This helps explain why the last building built on his watch, College Hall, was not appreciably different from the first. Only the mansard roof speaks of a changing world, and even that—making a convenient space in which to cram boarders—was a useful feature.

*   *   *

Rise and shine and give Chad the glory
He carries the freshmen in his bosom
He leads the sophomores by the still waters
He sends the juniors to the Devil
He charges the seniors for their diplomas.
—Anonymous

If any president could have brought Williams College into the modern world, it was Paul A. Chadbourne, Hopkins's handpicked successor. Having graduated as the valedictorian of the Class of 1848, Chadbourne returned in 1853 as chair of Chemistry and Botany. Having himself spent a brief and unhappy tenure at a theological seminary, he knew how to lead other would-be ministers to the world of science. He was instantly popular, and he helped push natural history to the center of the college's intellectual life. The building of Jackson Hall (1855), the museum and gallery of the Lyceum of Natural History, begun just two years after his arrival, was the first sign of this newfound energy. The peak of Chadbourne's popularity came in the summer of 1860, when he chartered a schooner and led an enthusiastic student expedition to Greenland.

As president of Williams, however, Chadbourne was distinctly less successful. Not the first beloved professor to turn into an authoritarian administrator, he startled the college with his strictness: "I do not believe in tolerating or ignoring the vices and follies of young men." Shortly after he assumed the presidency in 1872, he instituted a policing system whereby professors alternately served as "officers of the day," and although it was soon abandoned, he lost a great deal of the goodwill he had brought with his appointment.

Chadbourne was responsible for only two significant buildings during his tenure, and both turned out rather badly. In 1879 the college acquired the celebrated Wilder Cabinet, the valuable collection of minerals assembled by Lyman Wilder, an amateur mineralogist and polymath. Wilder's collection was installed in an eccentric octagonal house in nearby Hoosick Falls, New York, and Chadbourne wanted a building at least as distinctive. He began planning an

Henry J. Hardenbergh, the New York architect of the famed Dakota, designed the first Clark Hall in 1881. Built as the college's "geological museum," it was Williamstown's original Clark Museum.

Chadbourne Gymnasium (1882), "a slight, wooden, provisional affair," was built downhill from West College, near where Clark Hall stands today. It has the distinction of having had the shortest existence of any building at Williams College.

Williamstown in 1889, just before the massive building campaign of the Carter years that added Hopkins Hall, the Thompson Laboratories, and Jesup to the campus. Lucien R. Burleigh's commercial lithograph offers a lively image of the rolling topography that determined the course of roads and the placement of the first buildings, invariably placed on hilltops.

ambitious building that would consist of not only a geological museum but also an art gallery, lecture room, library, and rooms for the college literary societies. This was a tall order, but there was a willing donor, Edward Clark (Class of 1831), a lawyer who had made his fortune with the Singer Manufacturing Company, the world's most successful manufacturer of sewing machines. But Chadbourne bungled what should have been a simple exercise in fundraising. Rather than cram all these functions into one large building, Chadbourne decided to build several specialized buildings: one for science, art, and so forth. He fully expected Clark to fund all of them, but to his great dismay, the donor was annoyed at being asked to pay for another building and haughtily refused. Only the science museum was built.

This original Clark Hall (1881) stood until 1907, when part of its wall collapsed, forcing its demolition. Chadbourne's other contribution to the campus was even shorter lived. Unhappy with the gymnasium stuffed into the original Goodrich Hall, he secured a donation in 1880 for "a handsome new gymnasium for heavy gymnastics," to measure ninety by fifty-three feet. Completed in 1882, the barnlike structure looked insubstantial, and it was: just as the Class of 1833 was sitting down to their fiftieth reunion dinner, a freakish tornado swept through Williamstown and smashed the gym to kindling. But Chadbourne was

Frederick Ferris Thompson's original intention was to give Williams one enormous science building. But putting three very different types of laboratories under a single roof posed insurmountable practical difficulties. In the end, instead of funding one building costing $100,000, Thompson paid for three, each costing $60,000.

already gone; he shocked the college by resigning abruptly in 1881, dying little more than a year later.

* * *

In 1881 the presidency of Williams College fell to Franklin Carter. When his term began, Williams students had no say whatsoever in what courses to take, other than the choice of taking German or French during the summer term of junior year. There was no such thing as a major. Twenty years later, a complete system of electives had been put into place, including a series of science courses taught in modern laboratories. Carter also gave the college, for the first time, a stable and substantial endowment: he raised $1,100,000—a respectable amount when one considers that it was only $120,000 when he started. Finally, he presided over the creation of six major new buildings, each bringing significant changes to the life and character of Williams. It is fair to say that his presidency was one of the most consequential in the history of the college.

None of this could have been anticipated from the biography of Carter, the first scholar-president of Williams. His background was exclusively in languages. After graduating from Williams College in 1862, he returned three years later to be the professor of Latin and French. And with the charming elasticity of nineteenth-century academia, he went to Yale in 1872 to teach German. There he noticed Yale's introduction of the modern elective curriculum, and when he returned to Williams as president, he brought the system with him—and ran up against stubborn resistance. Carter could not liberalize the curriculum overnight; not until 1894, for example, was Greek removed as one of the subjects required for admission to Williams.

Besides an outdated classical curriculum, Carter inherited a woefully inadequate set of buildings. There was not even a proper set of classrooms: Goodrich was a hybrid gymnasium, chemistry laboratory, and bowling alley; the chapel had a pair of recitation halls tacked to the rear; and only Griffin functioned as an academic building. There were three aged dormitories, none of which had indoor plumbing, obliging their inhabitants to use outhouses.

Carter tackled each of these deficiencies systematically, moving with an alacrity and decisiveness that neither of his predecessors showed. To be fair, he had the advantage of generous donors. The first of his buildings, Morgan Hall (1883)—the first dormitory with plumbing and central heating—was the gift of Edwin Morgan, the former governor of New York. Carter next made good the destruction of Chadbourne Gymnasium by building Lasell (1886). Both buildings were by J. C. Cady and were composed as pendants to either side of Spring Street. For the first time in its history, Williams was arranging its buildings in artistic groupings, rather than merely placing them on the next best parcel of real estate.

Carter's greatest ally was Frederick Ferris Thompson, whose name graces more buildings at Williams than any other donor. His first substantial gift was Hopkins Hall (1890), to which he contributed the lion's share. Here at last was a modern administrative building, carefully planned, and although it mixed functions just as indiscriminately as its predecessors, it did so intelligently. Carter even saw to it that his corner office projected out, letting him keep an eye on his students (and his faculty, who gave him a good deal of grief).

The decisive gift was the trio of laboratories that Thompson donated in 1893. Here Carter succeeded at what Chadbourne failed to do: woo three buildings at once from a single donor. There could have been no more fitting gift to mark the college's centennial, a complete apparatus of modern laboratories that proudly declared that Williams was no longer a theological seminary, and that its mission was not to pass on old knowledge to its students but to teach them to generate new knowledge. Had Carter had his way, Williams would also have granted a bachelor of science degree, but here he failed, because of either faculty resistance or financial hardship.

Carter was blessed with his donors, but they were imperious men whose gifts came with architects attached. The results were mixed: Cady was an architect of considerable poetic imagination; his Morgan and Lasell are superb. By contrast, Francis Richmond Allen had not a speck of originality. He was enormously versatile—from the Romanesque Hopkins Hall and the neo-Gothic Thompson

Chapel to the Colonial Revival Fitch Hall—but it was the versatility that came from a cheerful lack of principle. With Allen one cannot help but think of Groucho Marx: "These are my principles, and if you don't like them—well, I have other ones." On the other hand, Allen was absolutely dependable and pliable, which explains why he built more buildings at Williams than any other architect. Only once did a donor's pet architect, George T. Tilden of Jesup notoriety, fail to deliver.

Carter presided over Williams College at the end of its Victorian phase. Typically, it was a student initiative that announced that great changes were underway. In 1893 a fire destroyed the Sigma Phi fraternity house; as always, the fraternity looked first to its own. Marcus Tullius Reynolds (Class of 1890), perhaps the first Williams alumnus to become an architect, had just opened an office in his native Albany. He had the bright idea of dismantling the Van Rensselaer family mansion and rebuilding it in Williamstown as the new fraternity house. Reynolds had been raised by his aunt, his father's sister, who married the head of the Van Rensselaer clan, the most consequential family of upstate New York. Having grown up with his Van Rensselaer cousins, he was able to persuade them to let him save the house and give it a new life in a new place.

What is remarkable about the whole affair is the light it casts on the changing attitude toward the past. Colonial history now seemed more inspiring than frantic Victorian invention, and the rebuilding of the Van Rensselaer mansion (1894) directly behind Hopkins Hall suddenly made that building, scarcely four years old, look dated. This was the coming of the Colonial Revival, which came to dominate the building activity of Carter's enterprising successor. The college's most distinguished economist, Arthur Latham Perry, regarded Carter with venomous loathing. Those interested in a dissenting view of

LEFT The peripatetic Van Rensselaer House (1765) was given a Renaissance facade (1843) by Richard Upjohn, and then moved from Albany to Williamstown in 1894 to become the Sigma Phi fraternity house, as shown here. Its eventful life came to an end when it was demolished to make room for Sawyer Library (which stood from 1975 to 2015). RIGHT Fraternities often chose more interesting architects than those chosen by the college trustees. James G. Cutler's disciplined design for Sigma Phi (1883) gives no hint of his restlessness: he went on to serve as mayor of Rochester and to invent the mail chute for tall office buildings.

the Carter presidency must read Perry's shocking account in *Williamstown and Williams College: A History* (1904). In the long annals of academic viciousness, it deserves a place of honor.

*   *   *

Henry Hopkins brought a proprietary feeling to the campus and its buildings, and understandably so. He was a son of Williams's most famous president and had spent his entire youth in and around the college, from which he graduated in 1858. When he assumed the presidency in 1902, he had been away for four decades. After graduation he was ordained a Congregationalist minister, served as a Civil War chaplain, and spent twenty-two years as a pastor of a church in Kansas City. Returning to a campus in the midst of furious change, academically and physically, his first step was to commission a campus plan for Williams, the first in its history.

Ostensibly, the reason for hiring a planner was to find a site for the new Thompson Memorial Chapel. The old piecemeal approach to siting buildings would no longer do; the Thompson laboratories showed how a coordinated array of buildings could create a pleasant and attractive quadrangle. Moreover, Hopkins knew that new dormitories were needed—half of Williams College students still lived off campus, a growing number in fraternities—but before building, he wanted a comprehensive plan. This sort of thinking was in the air. The Chicago Columbian Exhibition of 1893 had introduced America to the idea of large-scale planning, with both formal axes and landscaped parks. The planner of that exhibition, Frederick Law Olmsted, had recently died, but his firm, under the direction of his two sons, still existed. And so even before Hopkins was inaugurated as president, he summoned the Olmsted brothers to the campus to advise him where and how to build.

The Olmsted report, submitted on April 28, 1902, did not mince words:

> The thoughtful visitor is puzzled, not to say dazed, by the obtrusive incongruity of some of the more recent additions to the group of College buildings, and must find it difficult not to infer that there are two or more rival institutions each challenging attention to their business-like push and energy in keeping up with the newest fashion in colored brick and mortar to be found in the most strenuously progressive cities.

The Olmsteds noted dryly that buildings appeared in every color and material imaginable—red brick, bluish white limestone, light yellow brick, and brownstone, along with a president's house in wood—in short, "artistic chaos." They correctly guessed that it was the donors who selected the architects, each of whom assiduously worked to distinguish his work from its neighbors. The only answer to this was for the college trustees "to determine upon certain building materials and certain limitations as to style," and to stick with them, even at the risk of losing a donor. What that material should be, they left up to the college (although they put in a plea for the rugged dolomite of Morgan and Lasell, pointing out that it is always preferable to use local stone).

But one could not conjure up a new architectural style out of thin air; existing buildings had to be taken into account. You should not, for example, plop an ornate Decorated Gothic chapel next to a building like Hopkins with "tremendous round arches in the Romanesque style." (In fact, the college would do just that.) If stylistic variety was unavoidable, the answer was to use the simplest version of each style, while a common choice of building stone would do much to smooth the incongruity.

Hopkins asked the Olmsteds to consider the possibility of grouping the new buildings in a series of quadrangles opening onto Main Street. The Olmsteds embraced the idea enthusiastically. A science quad was already in place and only needed a building on Hoxsey Street to complete it. And the line of East and South Colleges could be duplicated to make the Berkshire Quadrangle (although they recommended replacing those dormitories with "much larger and more modern ones"). A quadrangle north of Main Street was a more difficult proposition, unless Hopkins Hall was moved back. But the First Congregational Church, still in its old-fashioned Romanesque incarnation, was a stumbling block. The Olmsteds gently suggested that the college might agree to buy the land and build the congregation "a new church, perhaps more conveniently situated for the majority of the congregation and no doubt much handsomer and more luxurious."

These were the immediate suggestions, but the Olmsteds also summarized the principles that ought to guide future growth. The administrative and classroom buildings should be at the center of the campus, and the dormitories at the periphery, where they could enjoy attractive views and fresh air. This segregated the more dignified academic buildings with their high ceilings and even ranges of windows from the more picturesque dormitories. These were to be enlivened by "bay windows, outside blinds, tower rooms, small porches, verandas, balconies, loggias, window hoods, small gables, dormers, chimneys, and eaves." Here the Olmsteds conjured up a vision of a Williams gone Gothic. It was not an unreasonable vision, since Princeton and Bryn Mawr had recently done just that (two campuses that the Olmsted report praised).

With Olmsted Brothers now the official campus planner, Hopkins went to work. To him the campus was like a neglected orchard, and he immediately started pruning. He first demolished that aged embarrassment, Goodrich Hall. Next, he restored or remodeled all the familiar buildings of his own college days that had grown shabby since the 1850s. West College was given plumbing, electric lighting, and steam heat. The President's House was updated, and the wall dividing the two living rooms to the east removed, making one elegant reception room. Griffin Hall was moved to the northeast, making room for Thompson Chapel, and in the process altered and enlarged. Finally, the old chapel was converted to a combined library-classroom building with "six new seminar rooms," and designated the new Goodrich Hall (1907).

Each one of these projects was handled by George C. Harding and Henry M. Seaver, two Pittsfield architects who practiced as Harding & Seaver. These were not glamorous commissions that would bring fame, but they were absolutely necessary to the college. (Ironically, while the architects would soon be forgotten, a young draftsman who worked in their office in 1907 and 1908 would soon win fame for his highly architectonic prints: Rockwell Kent. Did he perhaps assist on any of the Williams drawings?) Berkshire Quadrangle is Hopkins's most lasting contribution to the Williams campus. Postponing the decision to demolish East and South Colleges, as the Olmsted report urged, he concentrated on building the first new Williams College dormitory since Morgan Hall, erected more than twenty years earlier. Because this dormitory would demonstrate the new direction of Williams's architecture, its design was handled with unusual care. Instead of simply hiring the donor's architect, as in the past, Hopkins held a formal architectural competition, something the college had never done before. It was handled with great intelligence and probity, and there was even a professional judge: Robert S. Peabody of the immensely gifted firm of Peabody & Stearns (one wishes he had competed rather than judged). In the end seven designs arrived, of which several were published. All were Colonial Revival in style, which suggests that this was a term of the competition, implicit or explicit. The design of Allen & Collens was selected, although it was considerably simplified in execution. Still in the afterglow of the firm's success with Thompson Chapel, they would have had the inside track on the competition.

By now it was clear that East and South would remain, and Allen & Collens were given the additional task of integrating them into the new quadrangle by giving them their classical portals and also enlarging South (now Fayerweather) to match Fitch. Finally, a stone terrace was slung between Fayerweather and Fitch, defining the quadrangle to the south. One sour note marred this triumph of Hopkins's presidency. Even as Fitch was under construction, a frenzied wave of competitive fraternity building began, the results of which still stand on Main Street. This alarmed Hopkins for several reasons. These new chapter houses were much larger than their Victorian precursors and could accommodate a good many more members. If the fraternity residents spent most of their college careers living apart from their fellow students, it would lead to social fragmentation and be "unfavorable to the best college spirit."[6] He had a more concrete fear: that he would not be able to fill his new dormitories with students. In response he made an offhand suggestion calculated to get the attention of the fraternities: if any dormitory rooms went unoccupied, the fraternities were to be charged rent.

Hopkins did not live long enough to demand that rent. He retired promptly at the age of seventy, as he promised when he took the job, and just as promptly died. But in his six years of service he had done something remarkable,

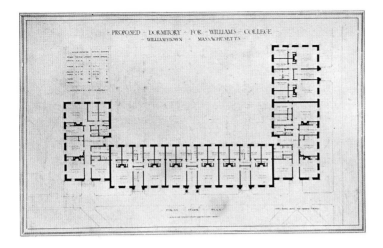

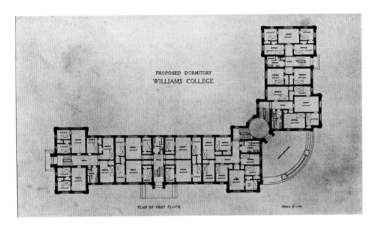

The seven architects who competed for Fitch dormitory showed considerable variety in their floor plans. Francis R. Allen (above) used the same repetitive order of his Thompson Laboratories, while J. C. Cady (below) reprised the picturesque irregularity of his Morgan Hall—a tactical mistake on Cady's part at a time the college was embracing colonial architecture.

which was to turn Williams College, which had been a motley affair of scattered buildings, into a campus.

*   *   *

James A. Garfield, the twentieth president of the United States, was assassinated in September 1881 in Washington, DC, as he was about to board a train to his twenty-fifth Williams College reunion. With him was his son, Harry, then beginning his freshman year at Williams. These circumstances guaranteed that young Harry would enjoy a special status at the college, which watched over him protectively through the years. When he graduated in 1885, it was inevitable that he would be chosen class speaker and praised for the "deliberate, manly, and attractive way" that he delivered his address (on the topic of socialism).[7] It cannot have surprised anyone when he was recruited in 1908 to serve as the college's eighth president.

Harry Garfield was only forty-four at the time, and he served until his death in 1934. This unusually long presidency gave the college some of its finest buildings, including an auditorium, a library, and three superb dormitories. Their quality was due in part to their gifted architect, in part to their open-handed donors, but also to something less tangible—Garfield's vivid and persuasive understanding of the social order that he wanted to create. He had taught political science at Princeton and was a friend of Woodrow Wilson, whose progressive views he shared. Garfield saw that the modern college was a different institution from what it was during his student days. Unlike the fairly homogeneous student body of the past, students might be much wealthier or much poorer; there were now great inequalities between those who had been educated at exclusive preparatory schools and those who had not.

Garfield viewed this inequality seriously, to judge by the policy changes he made immediately after returning to Williams. Any freshman who received a warning in a course had to pay him a personal visit, in addition to the customary daunting meeting with the dean. Garfield's goal was not to frighten but "to reach the student in a more general way."[8] He also instituted, for himself, the practice of taking his meals in Currier's dining hall, and he urged the faculty to do the same, to meet the students on an informal, social basis. Here they would establish a common gentlemanly culture and community, which would replace the ties of social class and religion that had once bound classmates. A crucial component of that new gentlemanly culture was architecture.

One year into Garfield's presidency, one of the college's wealthiest alumni, Alfred C. Chapin (Class of 1869), announced that he was giving the college a new auditorium building. Here was a test of the ability of architecture to shape community, and Garfield made the most of it. He quickly decided that the building should be the centerpiece of a new quadrangle, as Olmsted Brothers had recommended, consisting of a symmetrical array of dormitories. He was thinking of the Berkshire Quadrangle, with its ordered congregation of brick and marble buildings, similar in size and character. This was an ambitious program, and Garfield was fortunate in his architectural advisers. One of them was his younger brother Abram (a member of the Williams Class of 1893), an architect in Cleveland with a lucrative practice designing houses in Shaker Heights. While Abram offered occasional suggestions, Garfield's right-hand man was Bentley W. Warren, the college lawyer who headed the trustees' standing building committee. Warren was an old friend and fellow member of the Class of 1885, and in almost daily letters to "My dear Hal," he passed judgment on every architectural question. Besides helping Garfield select the architects, draw up the building programs, and choose the site, he critiqued the most minute of details, from the choice of stone for columns of Chapin to the benefits of planting English elms to the accuracy of a Latin inscription (was the infinitive form of *scire* acceptable?). This intelligent collaboration would have gotten fine work out of whichever architects they chose, but it was their good fortune to hit upon Cram, Goodhue & Ferguson, a firm of stupendous talents.

The architects had a peculiar working method: Ralph Adams Cram sat in the Boston office, where he worked out the plan and rough massing of each building, and sent them to New York, where Bertram Grosvenor Goodhue gave them their poetry of surface silhouette. This division saved the firm from archaeological preciosity and gave it creative tension. Goodhue, Cram once said, "never swerved from his vital originality, while I suppose I represented the reactionary tendency." By "reactionary" he meant *traditional*, which he evidently felt was appropriate for Williams. He kept the commission for himself, visiting the campus frequently. The first trio of buildings—Chapin, Williams, and Sage (designed 1910, completed 1922) was entirely his work. (By the time it came to build Stetson and Lehman, the firm had gotten so busy that Cram entrusted much of the work to his job captain Alexander Hoyle, his specialist in Georgian architecture.) For this Cram received a 6 percent fee, 1 percent more than the professional standard. He also stayed at Garfield's house when in town—an unusual privilege for an architect, but then Cram was regarded as a gentleman.

Besides Chapin, Garfield had another wealthy donor: Francis L. Stetson (Class of 1867), also a member of Alpha Delta Phi. In addition to donating the library that bears his name, Stetson quietly did a great deal to make the campus a more beautiful place. In 1903 he paid to move Griffin Hall to make room for Thompson Chapel; in 1908 he donated Smedley Terrace, the marble steps and balustrade at the south end of the Berkshire Quadrangle (now partly displaced by Prospect); and in 1912 he paid to plant four hundred oak trees that would make a picturesque path between the college and the train station. Stetson and Chapin's friendly rivalry to see which of them could contribute more to the college put Garfield in an enviable position. (Sometimes the rivalry could turn peevish. In Stetson's private letters we read him complaining about the site of Chapin Hall or warning not to begin construction until all the gift was in hand, in the event that Chapin die suddenly. More than forty years after he graduated, Stetson was unable to stop hazing his younger fraternity brother.)

When America entered World War I in 1917, Garfield was able to renew his relationship with Wilson. He took a leave of absence to administer one of Wilson's characteristically progressive initiatives, the Federal Fuel Administration, created to regulate the nation's coal supply. After the war, he worked to make Williams a showpiece of Wilsonian idealism, where representatives from different countries could meet and discuss the world's problems in a friendly spirit of cooperation. This was the impulse behind the

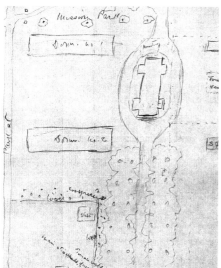

TOP "The scale of Grace Hall [Chapin] is somewhat finer on the sides than on the ends, in order that this dominant building may combine itself satisfactorily with the less monumental dormitories." So wrote Ralph Adams Cram, showing his characteristic sensitivity to proportion, which helps explains why the Freshman Quadrangle is easily the most attractive public space of the entire campus.

BOTTOM Cram's first idea for the Freshman Quadrangle showed a long alley of elm trees leading to Chapin Hall and two dormitories oriented east-west, without the L-shaped form they later took.

Institute of Politics, which was held at Williams every summer between 1921 and 1932.

Garfield imitated his progressive mentor in an even more ambitious respect. While president of Princeton, Wilson had launched a quixotic effort to abolish its socially prestigious eating clubs. He viewed them, quite correctly, as an obstacle to his program of socializing the campus along progressive lines. Wilson underestimated how furiously the eating clubs would be defended, and his campaign to group the students into separate colleges, or residential quadrangles, failed spectacularly. But Garfield was taken with the idea of separate colleges, and while Williams did not have eating clubs, it did have fraternities. And, like Wilson, he saw these independent and conservative organizations as an obstacle to socializing students for modern life. When it came time to build Sage Hall in 1922, Garfield made his move.

Rather than merely add one more dormitory in piecemeal fashion, as had been the rule, Garfield saw an opportunity to rethink the social organization of the student body. Sage Hall could be a component of a new freshman quadrangle where all members of the entering class would live, dine, and debate together:

> The objective is the creation of a sense of unity and a spirit of cooperation in discovering the best gifts of the members of each entering class.
>
> The dormitories, dining halls, and common rooms are but the outward and material part of the plan. The heart of it is the institution of round-table groups for the consideration of present questions vital to human welfare. [These discussions] will supplement the work of the classroom and the lecture hall.[9]

Clearly, Garfield was still enthralled with the early success of his Institute of Politics and thought its discussion format to be an ideal model for socializing Williams's entering classes. As attractive as this sounded, it required that freshmen no longer live in fraternity houses, which for the college was a radical proposal. To avoid the disastrous end of Wilson's proposal to abolish eating clubs at Princeton—which had been announced unilaterally, without any input from the clubs themselves—Garfield proceeded slowly. He took the extraordinary step of inviting all fifteen fraternity presidents to a private meeting on October 13, 1922, where he broached his plan for the first time.

Garfield was particularly excited about his idea for roundtable discussions, where groups of twenty-five to thirty students would meet weekly "under the supervision of advisors for the consideration of literary, scientific, political and religious questions and the student of current national and international problems." These discussions were to be conducted informally and conversationally, with no other goal than to "stimulate an interest among the undergraduates in humanistic problems." Garfield asked the fraternity leaders to send him written comments on each of his plan's three components: communal living, communal dining, and roundtable discussion.

As the handwritten letters trickled in from the stunned fraternity presidents, a distinct pattern emerged. There was great support for a residential quadrangle for freshmen and almost as much for the roundtable idea, although one writer suggested that it might be more rewarding to speak with seniors than freshmen on the world's problems. But the idea of communal dining met determined opposition. The upperclassmen, Garfield was told, played an essential role in "impressing Williams traditions and ideals upon the new men." It was at the dinner table that the callow freshman was taught manners, comportment, conversational etiquette by his older fraternity brothers. How else, they asked, was this to be done? Were the freshmen to mentor one another?

Garfield's challenge to the fraternities, although much less ambitious than Wilson's to the eating clubs, was just as fruitless. The reaction caught him off guard, and in the end he simply instructed Cram to build a mirror image of Williams Hall. His bold dream of a freshman dormitory, dining hall, and commons room was the last ambitious initiative of his presidency. After its failure he gradually withdrew into passive leadership, devoting most of his energy to his summer Institute for Politics. To recruit each year's participants was a time-consuming process, and each Christmas he sailed to Europe, not returning until after Easter. In the interim he turned the college over to his dean of the faculty, Carroll Lewis Maxcy, professor of rhetoric. This absentee leadership was not lost on the students, who made use of the dean's Hoxsey Street address (and what was then America's favorite soft drink) to make a scurrilous poem:

> Maxcy of Hoxsey,
> Prexy by proxy,
> Drinks Moxie.[10]

Garfield may have been a Wilsonian progressive, but he had one quality that his mentor lacked: a strong sentimental streak. It was his decision not to build an enormous new gymnasium on Cole Field, but to enlarge Lasell, already forty years old. And when he was told that the new college library should be built on the site of Lawrence Hall, the college library of his youth, he promptly vetoed it: "You know my feeling for the old Library," he told Warren, "hence it would go without saying that I should be opposed to removing the present building to make place for a new one." These two decisions were essentially sentimental—pragmatic progressivism has no reverence for the customs and objects of the past—and they ensured the survival of two of Williams's most beloved landmarks. In this an emotional component, however deeply submerged, must have been at play—and how could it be otherwise? After all, Garfield's whole experience at Williams was indelibly stamped with the assassination of his father, and a lifelong sense of intense, and perhaps even mystic, obligation.

* * *

Tyler Dennett was a man who spoke his mind freely, in pungent and memorable formulations, and had no use for the bland platitude—he was precisely what a college does not want in its president. The wonder is that he served as long as he did, from 1934 to 1937, the shortest of all official presidential terms at Williams. But he had a lively understanding of architecture, and had he served longer he would have had a far-reaching effect on the campus. Early in his term he identified seven buildings needed by the college—two of which, new squash courts and a new theater, we see in a student's daydream in a comic map of the college from 1935. (See p. 40.) Only the squash courts were built, and it would fall to his successor to complete his ambitious building plans, and only much later.

Dennett, who graduated from Williams College in 1904, was its last president to be a Congregationalist minister. Shortly after his ordination he switched to history and wrote a dissertation at Johns Hopkins University on US foreign relations. He subsequently worked as director of publications for the State Department and then became a professor of international relations at Princeton. He returned to Williams on a high note: in the same week he was named president, his *John Hay: From Poetry to Politics* (1933) won the Pulitzer Prize for the best American biography.

Dennett had decided ideas about improving the quality of the faculty and hiring young professors. Finding that there was no endowment to support faculty research, he promptly raised funds and created one. But he also learned that Garfield had granted tenure to a large cohort of professors near the end of his presidency, hampering Dennett's ability to shape the faculty. To remove what he considered "dead wood," he devised a direct method: he summoned the professors he wanted to dislodge to his office, one by one, and insulted them.[11] Most got the message and left. This assertive style, coming after Garfield's decades of benign neglect, was a surprise. Dennett was not only a devout graduate of the Union Theological Seminary but also a big brawler of a man, one who had played right guard for the Williams football team, missed only one game in three years, and did not flinch at a head-on collision.

Dennett was eminently quotable, and his talks were often reported in the national press. In one widely reported talk in 1936, he warned that the forces of modern life were tending toward standardization: "We have become more institutionalized at the expense of individuality and personality." In an age of political demagoguery, it was all the more crucial that students learn "the critical method," the habit of disinterested skeptical analysis:

> One of the indispensable conditions for study in an American college is an open mind. It seems unlikely that anyone who is officially committed to any political program to the point where he is not at liberty to change his mind as to the rightness or wrongness of a governmental system would profit from what an American college would have to offer.

Dennett was true to his principles. When it was announced by Nazi Germany that only students who were ideologically pure would be permitted to study overseas, he abolished the full scholarship that was given each year to a German student. Without an open mind, there could hardly be a critical method.

Dennett squirmed at the suggestion that Williams was a "socialite college," a term that appeared frequently in newspaper accounts during his presidency. Acknowledging that there was some truth in the charge, he condemned what he called the "appalling snobbery that has grown up in America in the last 25 years, which rules that one 'can't belong' unless he has gone to college." This bracing and unbuttoned quality of thought did not endear him to the trustees, who had grown accustomed to the sober Garfield, who did not think out loud in public the way Dennett did. The last straw came in March 1937, when Dennett gave a talk to the Boston alumni association where he said he feared that Williams

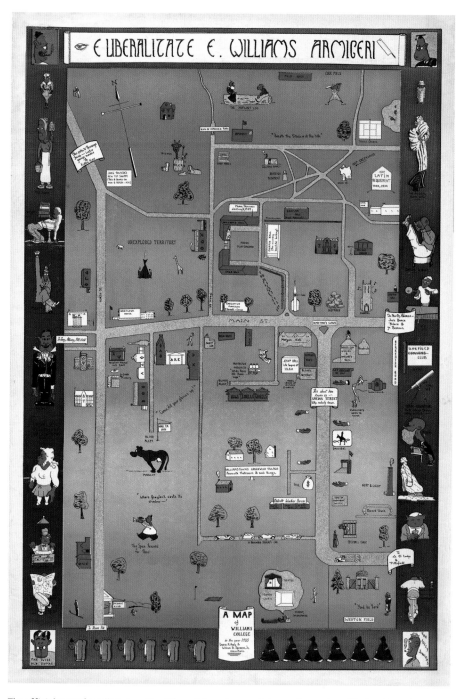

The official map of a college is quite different from the mental map of a student. The in-jokes of this student-created map reveal how much Williams has changed, and has not changed, since the map was created in 1935. Hopkins Hall is still a mound of rocks, and there still is no better shorthand name for Biology, Chemistry, and Physics than Bugs, Smells & Wheels.

College was growing less representative of the United States, because its students run "almost uniformly to the 'nice boy' type [who came] almost exclusively from 'good schools' like Hotchkiss, Kent and Deerfield."[12] His answer was to recruit exceptional students from elsewhere, which in practice meant from public and parochial schools. (In private he conceded that the college might have more Catholics, although not necessarily Jewish students.)

This legendary "nice boy" comment is what cost Dennett his presidency, although, as is always the case, a convenient pretext was needed. Matters came to a head over the Greylock Hotel, the roomy wooden hotel at North and Main Streets (now the site of the Greylock dormitories). The trustees decided to buy the property, in order "to prevent its falling into undesirable hands." Dennett opposed the purchase, arguing that the money was needed for educational purposes. When several trustees donated privately to reach the purchase price to acquire the hotel, Dennett offered his resignation. It was, he declared, a question of principle: was the college president the leader of the faculty and trustees, or merely their employee? In answer to his question, the trustees accepted his resignation. One wonders if they were aware that they had baited him successfully the same way he had baited the faculty members he wanted to dislodge.

The misfortune of Dennett is that he, for a Williams president, had an unusually rich appreciation of architecture. He valued the architecture of H. H. Richardson, for example, as a surprisingly sensitive passage in his Hay biography shows; this was hardly conventional wisdom for the time. And if he admired the genuine article, he knew enough to despise the counterfeit. He had Cram & Ferguson draw up plans for purging Hopkins Hall of its bastard Richardsonian motifs and remodeling it along colonial lines. It never came to pass and neither did his other bold dreams. Late in 1935 came a plan for a massive auditorium behind Griffin Hall, which would have doubled the size of the building. A few months later came a plan for building another transverse wing behind Lawrence Hall. Both were designed by faithful Harding & Seaver, and both were abandoned (except for a small infill project that added the Blashfield Room to the museum). These no-frills additions to existing buildings confirm that Dennett preferred to spend on teaching and research, not on flashy buildings. In the end, Dennett's one concrete architectural accomplishment was the building of the squash courts (1937), for which he singlehandedly raised the $100,000. The pleasure of making monuments on Main Street—such as the Faculty House and Adams Memorial Theater—would go to his successor.

*　*　*

The fall of Dennett required decisive damage control. What the college desperately wanted, especially after the laissez-faire presidency of Garfield and the ambition of Dennett, was sheer executive competence. A candidate was

By the 1930s Hopkins Hall was an eyesore or, as the art professor S. Lane Faison Jr. put it, a "romanesque monster." But it was too prominent and had too many historical associations to be simply swept away. President Tyler Dennett asked his architects to do the impossible—to turn the Romanesque behemoth into a colonial jewel.

found at short notice: James Phinney Baxter III, valedictorian of the Class of 1914. He had already been seriously considered for the presidency in 1934, but he was content at Harvard, where he was a popular history professor. He now accepted the position (reluctantly, by all accounts) and returned in mid-1937 to his alma mater, where he quickly proved himself an administrator of fierce brilliance. His twenty-four-year presidency is unmatched in terms of leadership—in a quality that one of his colleagues described as "savage intellect." It is easy to see why the Office of Strategic Services, the forerunner of the CIA, chose Baxter to head its Research and Analysis Branch during World War II. There he recruited some nine hundred scholars to apply their research skills to the war effort. Given these spectacular executive gifts, he might easily have changed the architectural character of Williams, had he wanted to. But nothing seems to have been farther from his mind.

As an undergraduate, Baxter had watched the construction of Chapin and Williams Halls, his formative architectural experience. Throughout his presidency, he championed the quietly confident architecture of the Colonial

Revival, as had his predecessors. He was supported in this by Henry N. Flynt (Class of 1916), the Williams trustee who played much the same role for Baxter as Warren had for Garfield, as the president's chief adviser among the trustees in all things architectural. It was Flynt who restored nearby Historic Deerfield, a small-scale New England version of Colonial Williamsburg. Under his guidance, it was inevitable that Baxter would bring Perry, Shaw & Hepburn to Williams College, the same architects who restored Williamsburg for the Rockefellers.

Baxter faced an irritation that Garfield had not, a younger generation of professors in the Art Department who were versed in the architecture of the Bauhaus and of Le Corbusier, and who opposed eclecticism on the grounds of principle. He ran into architectural controversy almost immediately. Cram & Ferguson's design for the Adams Memorial Theater, which was unveiled in 1939, pleased nobody: the *North Adams Transcript* attacked the "limestone structure of the so-called modernistic type" for its lack of harmony with the rest of the campus. The proper style for the theater was that of Chapin Hall. But S. Lane Faison Jr. (Class of 1929), the college's brilliant young art professor, disagreed, and in a scathing letter to the editor argued that fitting the space of a modern theater into a colonial shell would be "quite as ridiculous as putting a gasoline engine into a gilded state coach." (His letter was cosigned by Lawrence H. Bloedel, a fellow alumnus and heir to the Bloedel West Coast timber fortune.) Baxter evidently felt he had more to fear from public opinion than from his own faculty; the theater was revised in colonial fashion. Hoyle, Cram's classically minded partner, designed a light and graceful pedimented portico that complemented those of Chapin and the Congregational Church. This was Baxter's last significant act of architectural patronage until after World War II.

By 1947 Williams had returned sufficiently to its peacetime footing to think once more about architecture; unsolicited designs began to arrive. A major building campaign was overdue; the college had built little during the Depression and the war, and the sciences in particular were languishing in buildings more than half a century old. Architects were submitting speculative schemes, hoping to catch Baxter's attention. But before launching a capital campaign, he first commissioned his architects to draw up the preliminary designs he would need to estimate construction costs. On this basis he calculated that he would need to raise $2.5 million. In April 1948 he announced five building projects to which he asked alumni to contribute. With a sense of drama, he listed the projects in order of urgency: a $375,000 enlargement and remodeling of Physics; a $375,000 enlargement and remodeling of Biology, with offices and classrooms for Psychology; a $220,000 addition to Stetson Library; a $450,000 Garfield Club building and dormitory; and an $80,000 hockey rink. He also announced that the college enrollment would gradually be reduced from its current high of 1,100 students to its prewar level of 850, creating a more favorable endowment-to-student ratio.

The plan to reduce the enrollment alarmed students, who correctly assumed that it would result in higher tuition, and the campaign got off to a disappointing

Before Cram & Ferguson added a pedimented portico, their Adams Memorial Theater was in the modern classical style, the radically abstracted and distilled version of classicism that 1930s architects used for civic buildings—from Paul Cret in Washington, DC, to Albert Speer in Berlin. In 2002 the architect William Rawn cited this unbuilt design to justify his removal of the portico. Such is the long life of an architectural drawing!

start. As of November 1948, only 28 percent of alumni had contributed. This was a "dismal shock" to Karl Weston (Class of 1896), the college's beloved art historian, who played a large role in the fundraising. He observed that some alumni in the Midwest refused to contribute unless the college "silenced" its one outspoken leftist professor, Frederick Schuman (known generally, and affectionately, as Red Fred). With characteristic dryness, Weston noted that Williams had a faculty member "with whose utterances we violently disagree" and this had been true every year since 1793.

Some of the factors that delayed Baxter's building projects were unforeseeable, such as the Korean War and the resulting shortage of steel, and the fire that destroyed West College in 1951. But his greatest failure—his plan to build a Garfield Club—might have been foreseen, since it was the same one on which Garfield had come to grief and to which his own name clung like a jinx. In August 1946 Baxter commissioned Perry, Shaw & Hepburn to design a building for the Williams students who had not been selected by a fraternity during their freshman year, about 30 percent of the student body. The college grouped these students collectively into the Garfield Club, a pseudofraternity that offered its own organizational system, club officers, and the use of the common room in Currier Hall. Its members understandably felt themselves a distinctly underprivileged minority. Their second-class status was a source of growing tension at the college,

Williamsburg meets Williamstown. In 1946 Perry, Shaw & Hepburn proposed a Garfield Club building for Williams College, including a dormitory, dining hall, and commons room. Like their restoration of Colonial Williamsburg, it was quiet and tasteful, depending for effect on simple masses of brick, stone, and wood rather than carved ornament. It is a far superior design to the Baxter Hall they built six years later.

In 1952 Professor Whitney S. Stoddard was invited to review the plans for the new student center, which became Baxter Hall. He explained the objection of the Art Department to the neocolonial design and was promised that it would be changed. One month later he went to the Williams Club to see the unveiling of the revised design. Stoddard's verdict: "It was the same goddam building."

and Baxter's solution was to give them precisely what the fraternity members enjoyed: a building of their own. Over the next six years Perry, Shaw & Hepburn's design was revised—frantically and repeatedly—as the original clubhouse grew into a combined clubhouse and dormitory (1947), then a combination Garfield Club and student union (1951), and finally the freshman dining hall and student union that was ultimately built (1952).

To many, the Garfield Clubhouse was mere hypocrisy, a polite fiction that masked the exclusionary policies of the fraternities. The only proper solution, they felt, was for the college to compel the fifteen fraternities to accept all students. In the fall of 1951, this measure was put to the student body, which voted it down by a substantial majority (509 to 380). The college trustees themselves, invariably fraternity members, also voted it down. In protest, the Garfield Club decided it would no longer serve as a fig leaf for the college's socially exclusive policies and voted to disband itself.

Baxter responded with agility. He ruled that the practice of fraternity rushing be delayed until sophomore year and that all freshmen should dine together in a communal dining hall. This was in fact the reform that Garfield had first proposed thirty years earlier: a dining hall for the entire freshman class, none of whom would belong to a fraternity. Baxter Hall, originally envisioned as a Garfield Club, was realized in 1952 as a freshman dining hall and student union building.

Throughout the process of designing the new building, Baxter consulted the professors of the Art Department, but when at last they saw the completed designs in October 1952, they drafted a public protest. The letter, signed by every member of the department, began with an arresting condemnation of the architecture of the college.

> We believe that no distinguished example of architecture has been built at Williams College since Griffin Hall (1828) and the Lawrence Hall Octagon (1846), with the possible exception of the auditorium of the Adams Memorial Theater.[13]

Every other building at Williams College, as they saw it, was either a Victorian monstrosity or a spurious colonial pastiche—and it was a mistake to think that Cram's buildings were any less dishonest than their eclectic predecessors. Instead, the college needed functional buildings, designed by an architect who "accepts the challenge of contemporary problems and does not seek to hide them under a tasteful masquerade of the past."[14] This architect could be identified by means of a competition. They named MIT, Harvard, Vassar, and other institutions that were now erecting functional buildings. The implication was that Williams should abandon the practice of simply relegating its buildings to the most socially acceptable Boston architects known to its trustees, that is, those of Cram & Ferguson or Perry, Shaw & Hepburn.

The letter ended on a withering outburst against Williams's long afternoon of architectural eclecticism. The memorable and cheerfully venomous language was once again the work of Faison, then in his glory as art critic for the *Nation*:

We look forward to the resumption of creativeness in Williams College buildings after a very long, long lapse. When that moment comes, Chapin Hall, the Field House, and the front parts of the Adams Memorial Theater will seem very curious. Quite as curious, we think, as our chimney-stabbed Neo-Georgian heating-plant, the hectic romanesque of Chateau Hopkins, and the mournful dolomite fastnesses of Morgan Hall.[15]

As it happened, it would take another decade and a different president before Williams College built a functional modern building. But the criticism of Faison and his colleagues drew blood and helped ensure that Baxter Hall, which opened in 1954, would be the last of the college's colonial buildings. It stood until 2004, when it was demolished to make room for the Paresky Center (2007).

*   *   *

The presidency of John E. Sawyer, Baxter's handpicked successor, was one of the most consequential in the history of the college, not least in terms of architecture. In office from 1961 until 1973, Jack Sawyer oversaw more changes in the life of the college and in its architecture than perhaps any other president. Before he was elected by the trustees, he made it clear that he would accept the presidency only if the trustees as a group agreed to assume responsibility for enhancing the all-too-meager endowment. They agreed, and he took the job.[16]

The first problem Sawyer tackled was the deleterious effect of fraternities on college life. Baxter had tried to deal with some of the inequities in the system, but he had not taken the radical step of rendering fraternities useless. Sawyer initiated a study of the role of fraternities in student life, the *Angevine Report*, which recommended that the college assume all responsibility for housing and feeding students and for providing a social life, eliminating the functions that the fraternities had served. To that end, in early 1963 Sawyer commissioned a campus plan from The Architects Collaborative, the first such consideration of the whole plan since the Olmsted Report of 1902. The *Angevine Report*, accepted by the trustees in June 1962, required the college to take two steps: first, construct new dormitory and dining facilities that would create small housing units, similar to fraternities, to replace the fraternities as social and living centers, and second, transfer as many of the frat houses to the college as possible and use them to continue housing students.[17]

Newly constructed houses became Sawyer's single largest contribution to the architecture of the campus, particularly the Greylock Quad and the Mission Park Dormitory, big complexes composed of several smaller houses and located on the fringe of campus. In a wide-ranging interview, John Chandler, who had been on the faculty for six years when Sawyer took over and who became his first dean of faculty, told us that Sawyer cleverly used a model of the proposed Greylock Quad to further his proposal to sideline the fraternities. There was such strong alumni opposition to the idea that it was not clear that abolition would be possible without losing considerable alumni support. Sawyer invited alums to campus and showed them a model of the Greylock buildings to reveal his vision of the new Williams. More than a few recalcitrant alums were persuaded by the model to support Sawyer's intention: architecture in the service of social progress. With the Greylock Quad (1965), Sawyer replaced the very late, tired Georgian of the Baxter regime with buildings designed by Benjamin Thompson of The Architects Collaborative, a firm established in Cambridge by Walter Gropius, one of the principal European founders of the modern architecture of the twentieth century.

Sawyer knew that he wanted to turn Williams into a coeducational institution, but he realized that he could not do so until the fraternities had disappeared. To go coed first would have forced him to permit the founding of sororities. Once women started arriving on campus—a few pioneers matriculated in 1969, and the first four-year women students followed quickly—there was an even greater need for enlarged dormitory and dining facilities. Enrollment went up from 1,200 to 2,000 over four years. At first, 600 women students were added to the 1,200 men already on campus, in order not to reduce the number of the latter, a move that might put the quality of male athletic teams at risk. Women applied in such large numbers that only the brightest of them could be accepted,

Harry Weese and Associates, perspective view of proposed Sawyer Library (ca. 1970); Ben Weese, project architect. At this point in the design process, people objected to the proposed height. The architects lowered the building several feet into the ground, thus eliminating the entrance steps visible in the drawing. Instead, ramps led down to what would have been the original ground level, with the result that what should have been the most easily accessible part of the building, ground level, had no usable space.

if the 2:1 ratio were to be maintained. This discrimination against women who had higher GPAs than some of the men who were admitted could not stand. Gradually, over a few years, the enrollment rose to 2,000, the present level, with no restriction on the number of women to an artificial quota. Enrollment continues to mirror the gender ratio in the population as a whole.

Although the inception of coeducation was one of the most significant changes in the college's history, the impact on the campus was relatively minor architecturally. The number of women increased incrementally, as they were admitted one class at a time over four years. At that same time, the college was building new dormitories so that new spaces for women became available as they arrived. At other institutions, the shift to coeducation created problems of resentment when male students were forced into crowded living conditions to free up rooms for women. Unlike Williams, those institutions did not have the foresight to build new student housing. The only real architectural changes that the presence of women created were separate athletic facilities and single-sex bathrooms. The former was rather meanly handled in the beginning by a small addition to the gym. The administration at first solved the bathroom issue by housing women in entries in existing dorms that had their own separate bathrooms; the ends of Williams and Sage Halls parallel to Park Street served that purpose quite well. Over time, some students chose to establish unisex bathrooms so that men and women who were friends could live near each other in groups. That change seemed to occur almost without incident. An extensive program to light the campus to make it safer after dark added a needed sense of security, later enhanced by call buttons, marked by blue lights, that could summon assistance. Committees of students, faculty, and administrators continue to study ways to make the campus safe from assault.

Sawyer once confided to a senior faculty member that he could not afford to strengthen all the departments equally. He chose one department from each of the three divisions to enlarge: art, economics, and physics. To further the national and international reach of art history and economics, he backed the founding in 1972 of a graduate program in art history, offered jointly with the Sterling and Francine Clark Art Institute, and also stood behind the founding of the Center for Developmental Economics (1960), even before he became president. There young economists from third-world countries would learn to manage their countries' economic futures. Physics received no graduate program, but the sciences as a group profited greatly from the construction of the Bronfman Science Center.

An economic historian, Sawyer had taught at Yale before becoming president of Williams. He said that had he not become an economist, he would have taken up architecture. At Yale, he came under the influence of Whitney Griswold, whose presidency turned the New Haven campus into a hotbed of new architectural designs. Like Griswold at Yale, Sawyer brought his campus into the twentieth century architecturally. For starters, he gave Gropius an honorary degree at Convocation in the fall of 1963. The kickoff of the campaign of new buildings was the Driscoll Dining Hall (1963), an echo of Frank Lloyd Wright on a far corner of the campus. There followed swiftly the Greylock Quad, opened in 1965, and the Bronfman Science Center, inaugurated two years later. Both were designed by Benjamin Thompson, first a student and then partner of Gropius. Mission Park Dormitory (1971) by Mitchell-Giurgola Associates, a Philadelphia firm with strong modernist credentials, capped Sawyer's career as a builder of student residential complexes. The twentieth century was in its seventh decade when Sawyer began to accomplish this change.

Sawyer's final, and unfortunately least successful, contribution to the campus was the Sawyer Library, completed and named for him in 1976, after he had moved on to become head of the Mellon Foundation. Sawyer had the foresight to understand that he needed a thoughtful plan for the whole campus. Following the plan he ordered from The Architects Collaborative, written by Thompson, he requested a second from one of the most distinguished planners of the time, Dan Kiley. Kiley convinced Sawyer that he needed to build, at the center of campus, a new library that would symbolize the centrality of intellectual pursuits to the life of Williams. As it happened, the very center of the campus was occupied by the ex-fraternity house of Sigma Phi, which had a particularly interesting architectural history. Replacing the fraternity house with the new library allowed Sawyer to get a symbol of fraternity life out of the visual center of the college, and so Sigma Phi had to go. Kiley recommended Harry Weese as the architect for the library; Sawyer unfortunately took that advice.

During his time as president, Sawyer had to deal with student protests against the Vietnam War, as well as an occupation of Hopkins Hall, the administration building, by the Black Student Union, an organization that had come into existence, ironically, because Sawyer wanted to diversify the student body. He belonged, however, to the wrong generation to understand the needs of these new students, once they had arrived on campus.

* * *

After the challenging years of the Sawyer presidency, the college was ready for the quieter regime of John W. Chandler, 1973–85. Chandler had taught at Williams as a member of the Religion Department before assuming the presidency of Hamilton College, there gaining the administrative experience to become Sawyer's handpicked successor. He was the first president not to be a Williams alumnus since the days of Ebenezer Fitch and Edward Dorr Griffin. He arrived with the sense that the arts at Williams needed architectural enhancement. Chandler's contribution consisted largely of additions to existing structures, almost all designed by Cambridge Seven Associates. The Music Department for years had languished in makeshift digs in the basement of Currier. The department got handsome new accommodations in the Bernhard Music Center, adjacent to the main performance space in Chapin Hall. The Faculty Club had become overcrowded. Cambridge Seven supplied a commodious addition. The Theater Department, relatively new, needed an intimate performance space. Precisely that was erected alongside the existing Adams Memorial Theater, only to be demolished to make way for the '62 Center for Theatre and Dance. Computers were suddenly required for a modern educational institution. The interior of Jesup was remodeled to serve those needs.

The most ambitious additions planned under Chandler were to serve art and athletics. Although the Art Department faculty was greatly enlarged under Sawyer, he had not been able to improve its physical facilities, nor those of the Williams College Museum of Art in Lawrence Hall. During Sawyer's presidency, an accreditation visit to the college had suggested (with appropriate academic apologies) that the college's athletic facilities needed improvement. Sawyer had not been able to do that either. Physically, the two departments sat cheek by jowl in Lawrence Hall and the Lasell Gymnasium, both fronting on Main Street.

The Art Department faculty persuaded the administration that a single architectural intelligence should control the adjacent additions. In the search for an architect, Charles Moore, who had written a dissertation on water in architecture at Princeton, gave a presentation that fetched the swimming

Moore Grover Harper, aerial view of project to design adjacent art and athletic facilities together, late 1970s. Moore planned an entrance to the complex from Spring Street, with new storefronts opening onto a galleria passing between the squash courts and a new basketball court and swimming pool (middle right). The passage would have led to the enlarged Lawrence Hall, spilling down the hillside toward athletics. This would have been Williamstown's version of Moore's Piazza d'Italia, New Orleans, the poster child of architectural postmodernism that he designed at roughly the same time.

coach, Carl Samuelson. Whitney Stoddard, from Art and chair of the building committee, was already a Moore admirer, and so in 1976–77 Moore got the commission to design both facilities. Sad to say, a recession followed, and the college decided that it was impossible to raise funds for both projects simultaneously. Moore was taken off the athletics half of the assignment, and Cambridge Seven Associates eventually came to design that new building, which opened, bearing Chandler's name, under the subsequent president. Chandler had no inkling that the new athletic facilities would be named for him; the head of the trustees sprang the surprise in a public announcement that left Chandler stunned. The loss of Moore's joint project was unfortunate. One part of it was a proposal to connect Spring Street to art and athletics through a celebratory commercial galleria.

*　*　*

Francis C. Oakley, in office from 1985 to 1993, was surely the most ambitious president Williams College has ever had in terms of promoting the institution's intellectual growth. His desire when he became president, he said in an interview with the authors, was "to build nothing," a remarkable statement from a member of a group, college presidents, who almost always suffer from an edifice complex. A longtime member of the History Department and a highly respected scholar of medieval European history, he instituted a number of programs to aid faculty in their scholarly pursuits, including half-year sabbaticals after three years and financial support for research. The result has been a huge increase in scholarly output from a faculty that had historically prided itself most on its performance in the classroom. To further his support of scholarship, Oakley established the Center for the Humanities and Social Sciences, now known as the Oakley Center, in a handsome, early twentieth-century Colonial Revival house on the edge of campus. There, faculty on leave can have an office and participate in weekly discussions of their work with others who are enjoying the same opportunity to do serious work while remaining in Williamstown.

A major contribution of Oakley to the college was his drive to diversify the faculty and the student body, to foster a sense of inclusion of people of all backgrounds. The most important physical manifestation of this aspect of the Oakley administration was the construction of the Jewish Religious Center, designed by Herbert Newman Associates of New Haven, Connecticut, and opened in 1990. Never before had Williams constructed a building to serve a religion other than its founding version of Protestant Christianity.

Although the Oakley presidency intentionally did not include extensive building campaigns, there were some that resulted out of necessity. The college needed an up-to-date administration to deal with the complexities of contemporary life. That meant hiring new members of the administrative staff, who would need office space. At that very moment the Williamstown building inspector condemned Hopkins Hall, because it no longer even vaguely complied with contemporary building codes. To remedy that dire situation, the college commissioned Architectural Resources of Cambridge to design a completely new, code-compliant interior, as well as an addition that literally doubled the size of the original building (1988). Hopkins had once housed an administration of modest size, plus a considerable number of classrooms. The new Hopkins relegated classrooms largely to the basement, with most of the remainder of the building given over to a seemingly ever-growing bureaucracy.

The one new building of the Oakley years that did not conform to his no-building agenda was the Spencer Studio Art Building (1996), designed by the young Carlos Jimenez from Houston. Libby Wadsworth (Class of 1984), the daughter of an alumnus and trustee, Jack Wadsworth (Class of 1961), had suffered as a student from the hopelessly scattered teaching facilities of studio art. Jack Wadsworth, to remedy that circumstance, gave the money for the building and saw to its becoming a reality. Oakley agreed about the necessity of a single, unified building for teaching studio art, which was not completed until after he had retired from office.

*　*　*

Oakley's successor, Harry C. Payne, president from 1994 to 1999, did not enjoy a happy tenure at Williams College. He oversaw the renovation of Goodrich as a student center, which bears his name. Under his regime, the Simon Squash Center (1998), a very successful building, came into being at the urging of another alumnus/donor, William Simon (Class of 1973). Payne was charged with raising the money to build a vast new complex for science. He failed to find a lead donor, for whom the building presumably would have been named. Instead, the complex, financed by many donations, honors a Williams graduate, Edward W. Morley (Class of 1860), whose investigation of the speed of light in part undergirded Albert Einstein's theory of relativity. For a major part of the complex, the highly successful Schow Science Library, Payne did find generous patrons. Morley Unified Science Center and Schow Science Library, largely hidden behind Francis Allen's nineteenth-century laboratory buildings, opened in 2000, the year after Payne's resignation.

*　*　*

Morton Schapiro arrived in 2000, after the brief interregnum of Carl Vogt (Class of 1958), a trustee and lawyer, who generously gave his time to keep the college going while a successor to Payne was found. Morty Schapiro had taught economics at Williams before decamping for warmer climes at the University of Southern California. He arrived with the mission of making Williams nationally and internationally known as one of the foremost liberal arts colleges anywhere. In this he succeeded, as the appearance of Williams College at or near the top in the annual ranking of liberal arts colleges in *US News and World Report* year after year has demonstrated.

Schapiro presided over what is waggishly known as his *Grands Projets*—after the French president François Mitterrand's similarly named efforts in Paris—a vast new theater and dance building (a project he inherited from the Payne administration), a new student center, and a new library accompanied by a pair of faculty office buildings. For the theater and dance project, an architect, William Rawn, had already been chosen by the donor, Herbert Allen (Class of 1962), Payne, and a trustee. They had also selected a site at the south end of Spring Street. Schapiro told Allen that the theater could not be built on that site and even offered to give him back his $20 million. But they soon resolved their differences, and the result is the '62 Center for Theatre and Dance (2005), designed by Rawn and located next to the Adams Memorial Theater. The latter would have been abandoned had the previous scheme been carried out.

Schapiro knew that scores of colleges were building new student centers to attract applicants. Baxter Hall, the student center erected in the 1950s, was by Schapiro's time outmoded, and Morty (as everyone called him) was determined to replace it. He suffered, some joked, from Middlebury envy; a new student center at that college had impressed him mightily. Schapiro's solution was Paresky, which occupies the site where Baxter once stood. As a young teacher of economics at Williams College, Schapiro had been close to the students and understood the way they lived. The student center was only a part of his agenda to improve student life, which extended to his repurposing and remodeling of Sawyer's Mission Park Dormitory into an enclave exclusively for first-year students, who had been scattered around the campus after the college population outgrew Ralph Adams Cram's Freshman Quadrangle.

The third *Grand Projet* was a new library. Sawyer Library, never a great building, had become increasingly overcrowded with books and students, to the point that expansion was essential. Denise Scott Brown, a brilliant planner, was called in to consider what all the new construction would to do to the campus as a whole. Amazingly, no one had thought to ask that question. Schapiro speaks of her brilliance vividly; in only a couple of days she identified major planning problems that needed to be solved. She even took Schapiro around the campus to discover how students actually moved from one point to another. She came up with the concept of creating a pedestrian axis that would run parallel to Main Street to connect the Greylock Quad at the west to Stetson Hall, the college library of the 1920s, to the east. Her axial connection was in good part built but in a far less interesting form than what she might have designed, had she been asked to do so. Unfortunately, before Scott Brown could submit her report, Rawn's plan for the '62 Center had already been accepted, with its northern end blocking the path just east of the Greylock Quad.

Although the Scott Brown axis now unifies the north side of campus, the firm that she and her husband, Robert Venturi, ran did not receive the commission for the new library—even though she had convinced Schapiro of the poor character of the Weese building. Instead, that job went to Bohlin Cywinski Jackson (BCJ), who came up with the idea of razing Sawyer Library rather than adding on to it.

BCJ proposed a multistage solution. The Great Recession caused by the failure of Lehman Brothers intervened, however, and so construction of this multiyear project had to wait until money was available. It was completed only in 2014. The final touch, the landscaping of the new open space, designed by Stephen Stimson Associates Landscape Architects, was carried out in the summer of 2016. The landscape, with its infestation of marble slabs, variously dubbed "Falkhenge" or "Explosion in a Marble Quarry," has caused considerable consternation on campus, partly for its cost and partly for its looks.

* * *

Adam Falk, a physicist from Johns Hopkins, succeeded Schapiro in 2010. Before he resigned at the end of 2017 to take up the presidency of the Alfred P. Sloan

Denise Scott Brown was the first professional planner to attempt to tie the entire north side of the campus together visually. Her east-west axis comes to a splendid visual climax when its path passes between Sage (left) and Paresky (right) and focuses on the facade of Stetson, made visible by the removal of Sawyer Library. Her bold move demonstrates the possibilities that far-sighted consideration of the campus as a whole can open up.

Foundation, Falk instituted a vast, expensive campaign of building, ongoing at the time of this writing. His largest effort was concentrated on the sciences. Morley Unified Science Center was at capacity when it opened. For many reasons, students in the second decade of the twenty-first century began to flock to Division III courses, and by 2017 almost 50 percent of the student body was majoring in science, mathematics, statistics, or computer science. Of the twenty-nine members of the Class of 2017 admitted to Phi Beta Kappa as juniors, the intellectual cream of the class, only four did not have a Division III major. This student interest had to be accommodated, and new laboratory facilities to attract bright new faculty had to be constructed. The result is a large, new, currently nameless science building, mostly devoted to labs and offices, sited south of Morley, that will open in 2018. Bronfman Science Center, one of the finest buildings the college ever built, will be razed in the same year, to be replaced by a larger structure that will house the departments of Geoscience, Mathematics, and Psychology.

Under Falk, the college administration has sought to succor the commercial life of Spring Street by building a new Williams Bookstore on the corner of Spring and Walden Streets, and a new Williams Inn in Dennison Park at the southern end of the street. A project to build additional facilities for Art did not come to fruition because of an inability among the interested parties to agree on a site. Thus the college lost the chance to have a building designed by a major architect, Steven Holl, who had been engaged to study possible locations. It is too early to assess the still-incomplete architectural contributions of the Falk years, many of which were still under construction in 2018.

*   *   *

The Williams campus, over its roughly 225-year history, grew episodically, each addition placed by a decision made ad hoc, each building expressing the style of its day according to the talents of its designer, and each episode marked by a more or less successful attempt to take into account the existing condition into which it was to be inserted. The deep lawn in front of Chapin Hall and the newly created Library Quad, the visual heart of the campus, exemplify the episodic manner in which the architecture of Williams has come to be. Almost all the college's presidents over roughly the last hundred years have had a hand in creating this ensemble.

By the end of the twentieth century all available land at the center of the campus was occupied. If new structures were to be built, old ones would have to come down. Thus Williams began to consume its own architectural history at an accelerated pace. Paresky replaced Baxter, which in turn had taken over land devoted to tennis courts. The Library Quad presents a vast open space where Sawyer Library once stood and, before Sawyer, two successive Sigma Phi fraternity houses. Schapiro and Hollander were built with the knowledge that Sawyer, packed in between them, would come down. Behind this present state is a history of erections, demolitions, and changes of functions. Curiously, the visual cacophony of the area today owes its beginnings to the single best-planned episode in the college's history: Cram's Chapin Hall and freshman dormitories, Williams and Sage. The Garfield presidency marks one of the high points of architectural history here. Cambridge Seven's sympathetic addition to Chapin comes next, built decades later under Chandler; its relative simplicity and recessiveness pays homage to Cram's authoritative portico while deliberately avoiding its symmetry.

Paresky tries hard to integrate itself into the Cram–Cambridge Seven grouping by imitating the colors of the two and by assiduously lining the horizontal of its porch roof with the cornices of Sage and Chapin. Whereas Cram brought the classicism of Georgian England into the portico of Chapin, Ennead Architects (formerly Polshek Partners), the architects of Paresky, introduced the abstract, asymmetrical language of Le Corbusier's portico of the Assembly Building at Chandigarh, India, of the 1960s. Both firms chose as their sources buildings in which debates take place. It is not clear if this was fortuitous or planned, or if, in the minds of the architects, the functions of the sources had any connection to the buildings at Williams.

The void between Paresky and Sage reminds us of the unsatisfactory execution of the plan by Scott Brown, produced for Schapiro, to unify the entire north side of the campus with an axis running from Thompson's Greylock Quadrangle to Cram's Stetson Library. West of Park Street, in particular, the axis

In 2016 Stephen Stimson Associates, a firm of landscape architects, scattered remnants from a discard pile of a marble quarry in Vermont to create a mini mountain landscape below the Corinthian portico of Chapin. Strange as it may seem, this juxtaposition of the regular and the irregular, of control and chaos, has a neoclassical precedent in the architecture of late eighteenth-century France: Claude-Nicolas Ledoux's sunken garden filled with immense boulders below the portico of his Hôtel de Thellusson. Who woulda thought? Does knowing about the precedent change one's opinion of the design?

The center of the north side of the Williams College campus in autumn 2017, the last days of the Falk presidency, with the accretion of structures and landscape design of the past hundred years. From left to right: Schapiro, Paresky, opening of Denise Scott Brown's axis, Sage, Chapin, Bernhard, and Hollander, all seen from the west facade of Stetson Library. Sprawling across the west end of the quad and extending in front of Chapin and Bernard lie the stone slabs of the recent landscaping. Almost every Williams College president from Garfield on has had a hand in bringing this ensemble to life.

consists of poorly integrated segments of concrete paths and steps that in their lack of formal coherence recapitulate the episodic history of Williams architecture.

The only sign of the presidency of Sawyer, architecturally the most consequential of the post–World War II era, in this area is actually the absence of the library building that once bore his name. Similarly, the only memory of Baxter's tenure is the fact that the main gathering space in Paresky, the building that stands on the site of his Baxter Hall, bears his name. Sawyer Library was deliberately located at the heart of the campus to indicate the central role of intellectual endeavor in the life of the institution. What are we to make of the fact that that center is now a void?

Finally, Schapiro and Hollander now act to form a planned quadrangle focused on the front of the 1920s facade of Stetson Hall, another Garfield accomplishment. If one tries to identify historical prototypes for these office buildings, Wright's prairie houses incongruously spring to mind, especially in the deeply overhanging eaves shading strips of windows that sit on top of relatively solid walls. In this case, no consideration of the contextual appropriateness of the prototype seems to have taken place.

The ultimate element, chronologically, of the entire ensemble is the randomly cubist arrangement of blocks of marble by Stephen Stimson Associates, a completed part of Falk's architectural legacy. The landscape architects reached back literally into geologic time to celebrate the presence of a generally unknown vein of marble that lies hidden beneath the land of the quad. Their intention was to make us aware of a Williamstown that long predated human habitation, but, as is the case with much contemporary art, what is visible in the work requires a verbal explanation to make it comprehensible.

In the photograph's distance, rising above fallible works of human creativity, the monarchs of our mountain land proudly continue to stand. As is clear to almost anyone who visits Williamstown, the mountain setting, celebrated in the Williams alma mater, "The Mountains," its words recalled just now, is the constant in the ever-changing experience of the architecture of the campus.

1   The most comprehensive history of Williams College and Williamstown is contained in the two volumes by Arthur Latham Perry cited in the bibliography. They are crammed with information, but Perry almost never cited his sources. It would take a lifetime to try to track them down, assuming that many might still be retrievable. The volumes are poorly indexed, so specific subjects are often difficult to trace. The existence of both books online fortunately allows electronic searches. Despite their faults and their tedium, Perry's volumes are essential. Much of what one reads in this guide we would not know without Perry's tireless research. Published in 1899 and 1904, Perry's histories barely arrive at the twentieth century. The late nineteenth and first half of the twentieth century are covered in *Williamstown: The First Two Hundred Years* (1953), and that volume was updated in *Williamstown: The First 250 Years* (2005). Both are the work of multiple authors.

2   Perry's 1904 volume is the source of most of the early history of Williamstown contained in these pages.

3   Williams College Trustees' Minutes, May 23, 1792, preserved in the Williams College Archives, located in Sawyer Library, contains a copy of the Petition to the General Court.

4   Williams College Trustees' Minutes, August 5, 1793.

5   "Williams College Gymnasium," *Berkshire Eagle*, September 3, 1863, 1.

6   *Report of Henry Hopkins, President of Williams College, for the Academic Year, 1905–1906* (Williamstown, MA: Williams College, 1906), 12.

7   "The Garfield Boys," *Chicago Daily Inter Ocean*, July 1, 1885, 2.

8   *Report of Harry August Garfield, President of Williams College, for the Academic Year 1908–1909* (Williamstown, MA: Williams College, 1909), 7.

9   This reference and the following ones may be found in the presidential papers of Harry A. Garfield, Williams College Archives and Special Collections.

10 Told to the authors by their late colleague, S. Lane Faison Jr., who as a member of the Class of 1929 heard it (and very likely chanted it).

11 S. Lane Faison Jr., interview by Michael J. Lewis.

12 "College Has Too Many "Nice Boy" Type of Students," *St. Louis Post-Dispatch*, March 11, 1937, 15A.

13 S. Lane Faison Jr., Whitney S. Stoddard, William H. Pierson Jr., and Frank Anderson Trapp, "Letter to the Editor," *Williams Record*, November 8, 1952.

14 Ibid.

15 Ibid.

16 Williams College Trustees' Minutes, January 20, 1961.

17 The *Angevine Report* was accepted by the trustees on Sunday morning, June 10, 1962, just before commencement (Williams College Trustees' Minutes, June 10, 1962).

1   West College

Tompson J. Skinner and Benjamin Skinner, 1790; Remodeling: unknown builder, 1855, Harding & Seaver, 1904–5; Reconstruction: Perry, Shaw & Hepburn, 1951

Opened in 1790 to house the Williamstown Free School, stipulated in 1755 in the will of Colonel Ephraim Williams, West College became the inaugural structure of Williams College when it was chartered by the Massachusetts legislature in 1793 to replace the Free School. The name of a designer has rarely been attached to the structure, but, as Arthur Latham Perry pointed out, it was built and in all likelihood designed by the Skinner brothers. Tompson J. Skinner was a trustee of the Free School and chair of its building committee.[1] Skinner had been trained as a carpenter before he arrived in Williamstown in 1775 at the age of twenty-three, accompanied by his younger brother Benjamin Skinner, also a carpenter. The Skinner brothers, working as a team, were the leading builders of Williamstown at the end of the eighteenth century. They were responsible for the second Meeting House, 1796; the tavern (Mansion House); and East College. It was typical of the period for carpenters to design entire buildings as well as construct them. Tompson Skinner had a highly successful career in politics, serving in both the Massachusetts Senate and House, as well as in the fifth US Congress. His political career came to an ignominious end in 1807, when he was forced to resign as treasurer of the state of Massachusetts because of disastrous speculation with state funds in tracts of land in Georgia.

The trustees of the Free School had approved two smaller versions of West College before accepting the one we see today, but only after it was already completed. The final design was four stories, with the kitchen and dining room on the ground floor at the south end. Above these spaces was the chapel, a two-story room with a gallery accessed from the third floor. Also used as a classroom, the chapel had a platform against its west wall that provided elevated seating for faculty and tutors; the students sat opposite at a lower level or up in the gallery. Most of the rest of the building was devoted to dormitory space, with a small library off the central hall on the third floor and a room for a tutor on the fourth. The fourth floor also contained the room of the bell ringer. Stairs in his room led up to the bell in the cupola. He almost never dared to leave his room, because mischievous fellow students delighted in ringing the bell at off hours, if they could get their hands on it. No plans of the original interior are known.

A curious feature of the original West was that the town sidewalk passed directly through the ground floor. Because it stood across the town green, a public passage had to be maintained. This openness was remarkable, coming

scarcely thirty years after the scalping of three residents in 1796 off West Main Street, and it speaks to the rapidity with which peace took over after the end of the French and Indian Wars. The original east–west corridor through West College was wide enough to accommodate two men walking abreast, between two staircases that rose in opposite directions from the ground floor to the second. Above the second, only one set of stairs rose to the third and fourth floors. The building was heated by numerous stoves whose flues were connected to the four chimneys that rose above its roof. Water had to be fetched from springs to the southeast, and outhouses stood probably to the south. A lithograph published by Charles Currier, New York, and drawn by Eduard Valois is the earliest representation of the building, but its date is not clear. It does show the building before it was remodeled in 1855, when the doors in the centers of the long walls were eliminated. There are so many errors in the view that it cannot be entirely trusted.

Even if the Skinner brothers had not apprenticed with an architect, they surely owned pattern books to instruct them in proper principles of design. Tompson Skinner traveled frequently. In 1785–87 he served in the Massachusetts Senate, and he was in and out of Boston during the very years West College was being designed. Harvard, however, was not the source for its architecture. Five of the nine trustees of the Free School were graduates of Yale, and as Whitney Stoddard demonstrated in his classic book on the architecture of the college, Yale buildings were a major inspiration for the design of West College.[2] Perhaps Tompson Skinner visited New Haven to see those structures for himself, or perhaps he or one of the Yale-trained trustees sent for drawings. We have no evidence one way or the other. What is clear is that the design the Skinners came up with was remarkably subtle. The rows of nine windows in each level of the long sides are arranged in a pattern of 2-5-2, to break up the monotonous rhythm of the openings and to emphasize ever so subtly the central area of the facade. In recognition of the fact that the south end held the dining hall and two-story chapel, while the north end was devoted to dormitory spaces, the windows in each end were different in size and number. At the south were twelve windows, three per floor, that were five feet taller than the windows in the north, to admit more warm southern light into the public spaces. At the north end there were sixteen smaller windows, four per floor, to light individual sleeping rooms.

Most impressive of the Skinner details is the set of string courses that runs under the windows of each story. As the wall rises, the string courses grow one course of bricks closer to the bottoms of the windows above them, producing an illusion of increased height as the wall ascends to the shorter windows on the fourth floor, whose reduced height in comparison to those below also increases the apparent height

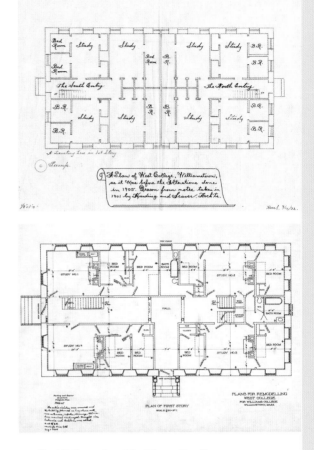

TOP **West College, plan of first floor, after 1855**
BOTTOM **West College, Harding & Seaver, plan of first floor, 1904**

of the entire structure. This degree of visual subtlety has rarely been equaled in any other building on the campus.

Before the construction of West College, there was only one brick building in Williamstown, the house erected by Captain Judah Williams in the 1770s, after his arrival in town and purchase of Lot 63 on the eastern edge of the settlement near the Green River. Williams's wife was an older sister of the Skinner brothers, who in 1775 followed her to the recently incorporated settlement. It would make sense that the reason they came to Williamstown was to construct a house for their sister and brother-in-law. They surely had other choices of places to establish careers. The construction of West required the presence of a brickyard nearby where suitable clay was available. That site, on the west side of North Street, just downhill from the intersection with Main, was accidentally rediscovered in the 1890s. The wealthy owner of the land at the time, Harley T.

Procter of Procter and Gamble, ordered it plowed up. The many hundred-year-old brick fragments that surfaced identified the brickyard's location.

The interior of West College was remodeled between 1854 and 1855. The doors on the east and west sides were walled up and new doors inserted in the north and south ends. A photograph made between 1877 and 1881 and printed by Gustav Pach, New York, shows the central windows in the long walls as pairs, which were almost surely inserted between 1854 and 1855. If the cupola shown in the Valois lithograph is accurate, then the enclosed cupola in the Pach photo was also added in the 1850s.

A plan, made by Harding & Seaver from notes taken in 1901, shows the reason for the insertion of paired windows. The east–west corridors were divided down the middle to create, as cheaply as possible, two pairs of long, narrow double bedrooms, each room lit and ventilated by one of the new paired windows. Each floor was divided into eight cramped, two-bedroom suites. The Harding & Seaver plan shows the ground floor, which must have been completely rebuilt from the original, which held the kitchen and dining room. The meagerness of the architectural changes in West was typical of the lack of interest in architecture on the part of the president, Mark Hopkins.

Harding & Seaver, in turn, rebuilt the entire interior during 1904 and 1905. Their plan for the ground floor shows four luxurious suites, each with separate bedrooms and a grand fireplace for pleasure rather than heat. Each of the two baths (indoor plumbing!) served two suites. On the exterior they inserted a new door with a fanlight in the south end, which still exists, and they also reopened the east door, flanking it with a pair of freestanding columns fronting rusticated door frames. The columns are no longer in place. By adding moldings to the top of the cupola, they changed its silhouette to something more attenuated. Elegantly proportioned triple windows replaced the old double windows.

In 1951 a catastrophic fire consumed the two top stories, and the brick walls bowed inward menacingly. Working from a plan by the Boston firm of Perry, Shaw & Hepburn, the contractor removed the remaining timbers of the lower floors, gently pulled the walls back into plumb, and filled the interior with the structure of reinforced concrete that now supports the walls (and rests on the original foundation). As the firm that had directed the remodeling and reconstruction of Colonial Williamsburg, Perry, Shaw & Hepburn was the logical choice to return West to something of its original glory. Their drawing for the set of cables and turnbuckles that straightened the walls states that the original first-floor windows remain in place. Perry also designed a new, open cupola based on the one in the Valois lithograph and replaced the columniated Harding & Seaver door in the east facade with a flatter portal that may retain the Harding & Seaver rustication. Neither doorway would have been stylistically possible in Williamstown in 1790.

2 Hopkins Gate

Fletcher Steele, landscape architect, 1927

Climb high, climb far,
Your goal the sky, your aim the star
—Inscription on Hopkins Gate, Anonymous

The Hopkins Gate ensemble takes one of architecture's simplest features, a flight of steps, and invests it with deep poetic meaning. The steps honor the two Hopkins brothers, Mark and Albert, who between them spent eighty years in service to their alma mater. For this, the college turned to another alumnus, Fletcher Steele, one of America's most important landscape architects. After graduating in 1907, he studied landscape planning at Harvard, where one of his professors was Frederick Law Olmsted Jr., who had drawn up the Williams campus plan. In 1914 Steele returned to Williams to landscape the grounds of St. Anthony Hall, his fraternity. From then on, he advised the college on landscaping matters and drew up a plan for the paths and plantings around Stetson Library.

In 1925 the college asked Steele to create a memorial to World War I veterans, but at some point (perhaps because the memorial function was taken up by Thompson Chapel) the Hopkins brothers became the subject. Steele had the apt idea that a memorial to dynamic educators should not be a static object but might suggest movement and progress. All the elements of the final scheme are present in a sketch of December 1926—a flight of granite stairs with a generously low rise, a pair of urn-topped piers, and a wrought-iron arch at the summit, bearing a symbolic lamp. At either side was to be a maple tree (now sadly needing replacement).

Steele made a point of consulting Mark Hopkins's last surviving child, Susan, who found among her father's papers the "Climb high, climb far" inscription, or so the story goes. This gave Steele his gentle pun: one literally climbed the stairs, but what truly mattered was the climbing that went on within. He made this clear by aligning his steps with the central axis of West College, which looms appropriately above the stair. To graduate, one must continue to climb and to aspire. This lifts the Memorial Steps into the realm of emblematics, which is the presentation of a poetic thought through a combination of words and image, and whose meaning depends on the interaction of the two.

Steele designed the steps at the same moment he began designing the sumptuous gardens at Naumkeag, the great estate of the Choate family in nearby Stockbridge, Massachusetts, which also offers a study in the lyrical treatment of a sloping site. As soon as the memorial was approved, Steele traveled to the Soviet Union, returning that spring to lecture at Williams College on art in modern Moscow—not that there is the slightest hint of Soviet avant-garde in the Hopkins steps; Steele was simply interested in everything. The steps were installed that summer and were ready to greet students at the start of the school year. It is not clear if they were more impressed by Steele's subtle steps or by the more radical change to the campus that summer: all the brick dormitories, which had traditionally been painted a cream color, were sandblasted and showed themselves in their naked brick glory.

3   Jesup Hall
George T. Tilden, 1899; Harding & Seaver, 1910; John Jordan, 1984

Jesup, whose garish gamboge fires the air of the whole campus.
    —Montgomery Schuyler, 1910

Has any building at Williams College lived as many lives as Jesup Hall, which has been a Romanesque-Renaissance hybrid, a Colonial Revival platitude, and a Postmodern essay in submission to the fire code and the Americans with Disabilities Act?

Jesup Hall, Williams College, Williamstown, Mass.

Although Jesup Hall was a Victorian straggler, built just as the Colonial Revival was transforming the campus, it could have survived its unfashionability had its walls not begun to fail, only a decade after its completion. For a modest $7,062 (plus $353 for the architects), the college was able to fix the building, both structurally and aesthetically.

Morris K. Jesup was a New York philanthropist who summered in Lenox, Massachusetts, and he looked fondly on Williams College, which gave him an honorary degree in 1881. He was also a former president of the New York YMCA (Young Men's Christian Association). In 1897 he offered to give the college a YMCA building of its own, provided that it raised an endowment of $10,000 to pay for maintenance. As was the custom in those days, the donor who gave the money chose the architect. Jesup chose the man who had designed his house at Lenox: George Tilden (of Rotch & Tilden).

Tilden thought carefully about the character of his building. In shape and materials, it related to the new science laboratories, but the playful features sprinkled across its facade—freestanding columns bearing lamps, a spurious attic balcony, a broad, welcoming porch—proclaimed that its function was not educational but social. Its key feature was an oversized sculpture of the college seal, specially cast by the Atlantic Terra Cotta Company, which Tilden placed above the rugged Romanesque entrance.

Within a decade every one of these features was swept away. Almost immediately the floor of Jesup's five-hundred-seat auditorium began to sag and, rather than summon the discredited Tilden, the college instead turned to one of its own, John S. Oakman (Class of 1899), who was then designing Currier Hall. Oakman underpinned the auditorium with iron beams, at which point the college decided that Jesup's appearance was even more of a problem than its shoddy construction, and what the building really needed was a facelift. This operation was given to the college's utility architects, Harding & Seaver, who had demonstrated their competence in the remodeling of West College and Griffin.

Harding & Seaver went to work with a vengeance. Off came the ventilation towers, the bizarre central dormer, the freestanding columns, and the misshapen rusticated arch; in their place came a graceful Palladian window and an understated recessed entrance. It almost (but not quite) turned Tilden's eclectic hodgepodge into a polite and tasteful Colonial Revival essay.

Jesup suffered an identity crisis once Baxter Hall opened in 1954. No longer the principal student center, Jesup was gradually taken over by the development and alumni offices. By the time it was converted to a computer center in 1984, and its auditorium removed, its origin as the college's YMCA building had long been forgotten, and the whole building's yellow brick walls given a coat of purple paint. In yet another round of alterations, the grand central stair was extracted, a pair of obtrusive fire stairs placed at either end, and a glass porch fitted around its entrance. One suspects that further indignities are in store.

ADAM FALK SCIENCE QUAD

4   Thompson Laboratories
Francis R. Allen, 1891–93; Allen & Collens, 1915, 1941; Des Granges & Steffian, 1950–51; Einhorn Yaffee Prescott, 1998–2001

I will build a series of three laboratories—chemical, physical and biological. The architect is to be F. R. Allen of Boston. They will probably cost over $100,000. I think we will put up about one a year, so as to have all completed for the college centennial in '93. They are to be called the Thompson Laboratories.
—Frederick Ferris Thompson, 1891

This pithy announcement set in motion the single greatest change to the character of Williams College. Frederick F. Thompson's gift went hand in hand with a sweeping change to the curriculum: as of 1891, the required courses in physics, chemistry, and biology were to be completed by the sophomore year "so that scientific elective work could be carried on for two more years."[3] And so on the centenary of its founding, Williams was to become a modern educational institution, no longer a seminary for turning out Congregationalist ministers but something closer to the research universities of Germany.

Aware of the ceremonial occasion, Francis R. Allen took special care to relate his laboratories to West College. Rather than construct a single monumental building, he created three smaller buildings, almost domestic in scale. Each was an affectionate paraphrase of West: a rectangular brick box with a hipped roof, a cupola above, and no decoration other than a portico around the central

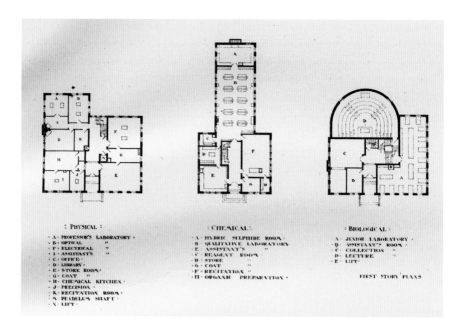

: PHYSICAL :

- A · PROFESSOR'S LABORATORY ·
- B · OPTICAL   "
- F · ELECTRICAL   "
- I · ASSISTANT'S   "
- C · OFFICE ·
- D · LIBRARY ·
- G · COAT   "
- H · CHEMICAL KITCHEN ·
- J · PRECISION ·
- K · RECITATION ROOM ·
- N · PENDULUM SHAFT ·
- X · LIFT ·

: CHEMICAL :

- A · HYDRIC SULPHIDE ROOM ·
- B · QUALITATIVE LABORATORY ·
- E · ASSISTANT'S   "
- C · REAGENT ROOM ·
- D · STORE   "
- G · COAT   "
- F · RECITATION   "
- H · ORGANIC PREPARATION ·

: BIOLOGICAL :

- A · JUNIOR LABORATORY ·
- D · ASSISTANT'S ROOM ·
- C · COLLECTION   "
- D · LECTURE   "
- E · LIFT ·

FIRST STORY PLANS

Francis Allen designed the Thompson Laboratories at a time when architects were split into two camps: medievalists liked to design outward from a functional plan, making a picturesque array of volumes; classicists placed a premium on order and symmetry, making balanced, disciplined compositions. Allen was too relaxed about style to be dogmatic and had no qualms about hiding the irregular plans of his laboratories behind classical facades.

entrance. Allen specified "rain-struck brick," a type with a pleasantly soft texture to suggest age (at just this moment he specified the same brick for his dormitories at Vassar, also funded by Thompson). The trim is of Warsaw Bluestone, an attractive and fine-grained stone quarried in western New York. Allen lined up the three buildings at the foot of the hill to the south of West, to which they look up like three dutiful schoolchildren gazing at their teacher. Here for the first time Williams had something like an academic quadrangle.

The three laboratories are only approximately symmetrical, midway between Victorian picturesqueness and academic formality. But to the rear they are wildly different. Biology is taught largely through lectures; hence it had a large semicircular auditorium. Chemistry labs are long and narrow, so they can be served by a single line of gas burners and hoods; they are also prone to fire and explosion, and are best separated from the main building. Physics had no great spatial requirements, but even here Allen created visual variety, playfully breaking up the volumes. This contrast between the polite facades and hectic rears was something that amused Victorian architects, who rudely referred to their "Queen Anne fronts and Mary Ann behinds."

When the science facilities were enlarged after 1998, the architects tucked their additions behind Allen's three laboratories, thereby maintaining their visual integrity. Only the Colonial Revival facade of the central building looks somewhat out of place. This is a later work of Allen, who was brought back in 1915 after—as he had correctly anticipated—a lab fire burned Thompson Chemistry to the ground.

That fire was a spectacular affair, the highlight of which was the sight of chemistry professor Brainerd Mears saving himself by sliding down the drain spout. But it also brought the college considerable embarrassment. The Victorian architecture of the laboratories was sadly dated at a time when the college had committed itself wholeheartedly to the Colonial Revival. John Oakman, whose design for Currier helped inaugurate the change, wrote to the administration to propose that he himself rebuild the laboratory, which should look nothing like "its too ugly neighbors." But this was the problem: the donor's wealthy widow was still very much alive and involved with the affairs of the college. However the chemistry laboratory was rebuilt, it could in no way suggest to Mrs. Thompson that her husband's original buildings were deficient. While a flat Colonial Revival roof for Chemistry would be fashionable, it would contrast jarringly with the high roofs of Biology and Physics. President Harry Garfield cautioned Allen to steer a middle course between contemporary taste and historical context. This explains what is otherwise a mystery: why an up-to-date Colonial Revival building carries that incongruous Victorian roof.

In 1947 the Boston firm of Des Granges & Steffian was engaged to remodel and enlarge the laboratories, but the distressingly slow capital campaign delayed the project until 1950. Physics and Biology each received a large brick addition, only to be swallowed up half a century later in the sprawl of the Morley Unified Science Center.

5   Bronfman Science Center
Benjamin Thompson Associates, 1962–68; Demolished, 2018

When the Soviet Union launched *Sputnik* in 1957, beating the United States in the Cold War race to put the first satellite in orbit, the teaching of science in this country was thrown into chaos. Why had we allowed the Russians to beat us? What could we do to recoup? The Bronfman Science Center was Williams's answer: an interdisciplinary center to coordinate the teaching of the sciences in a more effective way that was first proposed by a committee of faculty scientists and eagerly taken up by President Jack Sawyer as early as December 1962. A study for the project was undertaken in the spring of 1964 by graduate architecture students at Harvard under the guidance of Benjamin Thompson.

The north end of Bronfman Science Building was the architect Benjamin Thompson at his very best as a sensitive neighbor. The most formally symmetrical part of the building went brilliantly with the big Palladian light in the west wall of Clark Hall, making it clear that classicism does not depend on Corinthian columns. Thompson shaped a highly effective, angled vestibule to the science quad. In the bold projection just before the narrow opening to the extended space beyond, there was an intriguing echo of Michelangelo.

The site chosen was the western end of the science quad, where two late nineteenth-century houses stood with their backs to the academic buildings. The program for the new building called for a large structure that, if not carefully designed, could overwhelm the quad and even the entire campus. Thompson's brilliant solution was to break the apparent size of the building down into asymmetrical masses that advance and recede on both the east and west sides. He integrated the new with the old in a masterful way. The traditional structure of brick walls with granite lintels over the windows in Francis Allen's science buildings was picked up in the broad concrete lintels resting on the brick walls of Bronfman. The brick was a visually integrating veneer over reinforced concrete walls that were necessary to bear the loads of the wide ceiling spans required by large lab spaces and the weight of their equipment.

The only continuous horizontal in the exterior of the building was a heavy concrete cornice that put a lid on the building against the sky and connected Bronfman visually with the biology building to its south and Clark Hall, the geology building, to the north—a smart visual move for an interdisciplinary science building to make. In the Trustees' Minutes of April 1965, that cornice was the subject of a rare entry (the minutes almost never contain mention of architectural forms): "The building has been considerably lowered on the site in relation to the cornices of Clark Hall and Thompson Biology Laboratory since the original plan for the building was submitted. This has noticeably helped to reduce the sense of mass on the site in relation to these adjoining buildings."[4] Sawyer's eye was surely at work here. On its east side, Bronfman advanced to meet Biology, receded in its center to embrace the entrance, and then moved forward slightly to approach Geology, leaving an open space between the two to allow views into the distance. Bronfman was a superb lesson in how to make a new building, uncompromising in its modernity, fit into an old situation. Whitney Stoddard, the Art Department's celebrated teacher of modern architectural history, judged it "our finest 'big' building."[5]

The program called for a large auditorium and a series of psychology labs that did not fit easily into this scheme. Thompson hid the auditorium underground, below the northern wing of the building, and put the labs into a tower tucked behind the south end, where it was not visible from the quad, although it loomed over domestic-scaled Hoxsey Street. The north end became the "dry" part of the building, with the auditorium, classrooms, and a two-story library originally shared by Mathematics and Psychology. The library was one of the best "modern" spaces on campus, with expansive views north toward Main Street through a two-story wall of glass extended in a dramatic cantilever from the main mass. The receding center was devoted to circulation spaces, while the south end was the "wet" part, containing labs. A delightful surprise on the top floor of the south wing was the circular skylights, painted taxi-cab yellow, that emphatically brought the color of the sun down into narrow corridors on gloomy winter days. The colors Thompson used inside were the intense ones of

Pop Art, the hottest thing in the art world when Bronfman was new. There were splendidly vivid contrasts, such as the glowing bottle green of the projection booth against the intense orange of the carpet and seats in the auditorium.

6   North Science Building
Payette, 2020

The replacement for Bronfman had a hard act to follow, and it took more than one try, over two years, 2016–17, to get it right. Because Bronfman had been built in an era of extraordinarily low-cost energy, it had become enormously expensive to heat. Its bearing-wall structure could not be modified to accommodate new spatial needs and new ways of teaching science. The new design shrewdly adopts the notion of breaking the building up into separate masses to diminish its apparent size.

It houses, from north to south, the departments of Mathematics, Psychology, and Geosciences—the whole is divided into three parts, one for each discipline, with a bit of occasional overlap. Each department has its own window on the world: Math toward Main Street, Psych toward the science quad, and Geos toward Hoxsey Street. The apparent size is further diminished by a playfully irregular repetition of two window sizes that enliven the facade and give it a delightfully humane scale. The brick continues the traditional materials of the quad, and the flat roof maintains the general building height of the older structures. Ground has not been broken for the still-unnamed north building, so the character of the interior cannot be described beyond noting that both Math and Psych will have two-story social spaces around which faculty offices are gathered.

7   Clark Hall
Frank E. Wallis, 1907–8

> The building is very pure Colonial, much more so than most of the modern adaptations of that style, but is, nevertheless, very sincere and straightforward in design, and without the dryness and hardness which it is usually impossible to disassociate from work so archaeological.
> —*Architecture* (August 1909)

The Clark Art Institute is not the first museum in Williamstown created by the Clark family. In September 1880 Williams College was given a "geological museum" by Edward Clark (Class of 1831), lawyer and president of the Singer Manufacturing Company. Edward Clark was the grandfather of Sterling Clark, who later created the Clark Art Institute. Edward Clark was heavily involved in New York real estate development, and his projects include the famous Dakota Apartments (where

John Lennon lived and was shot). All were by the same architect, Henry J. Hardenbergh, who also designed Williams College's original Clark Hall, regarded as the first Clark museum.

Until 1907, when part of its wall collapsed, that building stood on what would later be the site of Currier Hall. Edward Clark himself had died in the meantime, but his daughter-in-law and four grandsons agreed to pay for an entirely new building on another site. This move was in accordance with the report of the Olmsted brothers, who had recommended that the Berkshire Quadrangle be reserved for dormitories and that buildings devoted to the sciences cluster around the new Thompson Laboratories. The rather odd location of the new Clark Hall, which seems aligned with nothing else, stands off by itself, like someone waiting politely at the edge of a conversation, hoping to be invited in.

When the present Clark Hall was dedicated in 1908, President Garfield noted approvingly how it "conforms with the architectural type of the older buildings on the campus," by which he meant West College. This helps explain why the commission was given to Frank E. Wallis, a Colonial Revivalist of the first rank. Wallis had a difficult sloping site, which he dealt with by putting the north entrance at the second-story level and the south entrance a story lower. While he deferred to the late Georgian language of West College, he made subtle adjustments to avoid its boxiness. The building is tucked into the hillside and the ground floor treated like a base so that it suggests a two-story building. And the end bays project slightly, accentuating the ends and breaking up the mass of the building.

The persnickety professional journal *Architecture* had nothing but praise for the building. It applauded the door ("a very delightful piece of architecture... with the lightness and grace of the best Colonial work"), the treatment of the skylight and roof ("unusual and brilliant"), and even the delicately wrought frieze (instead of striving for false French "virility," it combines "delicacy of scale... with the utmost strength of proportion").[6]

Clark Hall is oddly sited, standing neither on Main Street nor on Hoxsey Street, but somewhere in between. Wallis seems to have been concerned about making a smooth transition between the domestic architecture of Fraternity Row and the stately formality of West College. If that was his objective, he achieved it nimbly: the cupola and dignified character link Clark to West College on one side, while its compact size and clublike air relate to the fraternities on the other. Here the subject of geology presents itself as a kind of gregarious but somewhat detached fellowship, which in fact it is.

8   Jenny Holzer, *715 molecules*, 2011, sandblasted norite
Williams College Museum of Art, gift of the friends of J. Hodge Markgraf, Class of 1952, Ebenezer Fitch Professor of Chemistry

Thoughtfully sited so that it pointed to a now-dead maple tree (recently replaced), not to the building of a specific discipline, Jenny Holzer's green stone table engraved with chemical symbols is meant for use by the whole quad or indeed anyone who comes along and decides to sit down.

Holzer is famous for her combination of sculptural forms and language. Here she uses a scientific language, no more accessible to those who do not know it than, say, Russian is to those ignorant of the Cyrillic alphabet. The choice of specific molecules was not random. Some were personally important to Hodge Markgraf, who taught chemistry at Williams for many years with great success, for his own research. Others refer playfully to student life (e.g., caffeine molecule, nicotine molecule, alcohol molecule, and even the sex pheromone of the gypsy moth). Still others cast a sobering light on the history of the twentieth century, such as the molecules that comprise DDT, TNT, and mustard gas. Finally, it is fascinating how long chains of molecules with repetitive structure fit into the narrow edges of the slabs. As is almost always the case with Holzer's work, the table raises more questions than it answers. What could be more appropriate for an educational institution? Sit and let the table work its magic on your intellect.

The table was given in memory of Markgraf by colleagues and former students. He and Holzer were intellectual friends, a fact that makes this work a particularly fitting tribute.

9   Morley Unified Science Center
Zimmer Gunsul Frasca / Einhorn Yaffee Prescott, 2000

As education in the sciences came to be more and more important at Williams, the need for additional laboratory, classroom, and study spaces, as well as a separate science library, became acute. Morley Unified Science Center, named for a distinguished nineteenth-century teacher of physics, Edward W. Morley, whose work anticipated Albert Einstein's (no donor came forward to claim naming rights with a substantial gift), was the solution, although not for long (see below). It is an enormous addition to the south of the Francis Allen buildings, which largely conceal its bulk from the science quad. Visible from that crucial open space on the campus are only the black glass fragments that betray the new roofscape. As a local wag put it, "The best thing about this building is that you can't see it." The only real intrusion on the quad is the shadowy, black glass entrance to the complex, wedged between Physics and Chemistry. If it were not for the gleaming metallic doors, one would hardly know that the new entrance exists.

The building has enjoyed ample success in terms of the library spaces, beloved by students, and of the laboratory spaces. The new entrance from the quad leads into an area known as the Eco Cafe, where students and faculty can gather in a winter-garden environment to talk over coffee. As an entrance to the entire complex, this area offers no clear path to the various parts. Signage, always an admission of architectural failure, directs the lost to the library. Downstairs there is a large lecture hall, the Wege Auditorium, but you have to

Eco Cafe, Morley Unified Science Center

know from past experience where it is to find it again. Once the library is gained, the wanderer is treated to the most interesting part of the structure: the four-story interior lit by angular skylights that dance overhead. The contrast between the rough-textured brick walls of the earlier science buildings with the cream-colored, smooth planes of the new construction enhances the effect of both.

One of the most difficult parts of the assignment for the architects was to make the entire structure handicapped accessible. They connected the three old Francis Allen science buildings with a continuous path that becomes something of a roller coaster joining the varying floor levels of the separate structures. Much of the rest of the interior is a maze in which even the most well-traveled visitors can easily get lost.

The one part of the exterior that is easily visible is the southeast corner, reachable from Spring Street. Here one finds a memorable architectural anticlimax. Greeting the visitor is a gleaming concrete porch, with two hefty concrete columns that support a terrace. Set under the terrace are black glass walls with another shiny pair of metallic doors. If ever architectural

Schow Library

forms said, "Enter here," these do. So one enters, into a cramped cul-de-sac, face-to-face with glass vitrines that display a few historical specimens of scientific apparatuses. Almost never is someone studying them. A fire stair offers escape, but it is not clear where it leads. If in frustration one retreats to the outdoors, nearby one finds a sign that says it is impossible to get into the library from here. Go around to the front.

10 New South Science Building
Payette, 2015–18

When Morley opened, it was already at capacity. In the meantime, interest in science among undergraduates has surged, so as of this writing, almost

half the student body majors in a subject included in Division III, Science and Mathematics. The old spaces simply became inadequate to house the expanding enrollments and a growing faculty. Planning for the building started in 2013–14. Payette was hired because the firm specializes in science centers. The emphasis was on function more than architectural design.

The project grew to the point where it had to be split into two parts: labs, faculty offices, and student study spaces to the south, and, replacing Bronfman, a building to house Geosciences, Mathematics, and Psychology to the north. The labs are housed in a vast rectangular solid that parallels Walden Street. Connecting this slab to Morley is a wing that runs at right angles to it, creating an L that houses offices and study rooms. The South Building contains at least thirty laboratories, with adjacent service spaces. The labs, intended to be flexible to accommodate the unpredictable, fast-moving nature of scientific research, are designed to attract the best young faculty, who are engaged in pathbreaking work. They are also designed to be used by students, who labor alongside faculty: the driving concept is that students have to do science to learn science.

The terra-cotta skin of the lab building, imported from Germany, is one of its most interesting features. The rectangular panels, scored with parallel incisions that come in three different widths, seem at times to be three related but different colors. The actual color of all three types of panels is identical, and on sunless days they all look the same. The scoring responds to light in such diverse ways, however, that in direct sunlight the panels appear to be three distinct, randomly applied colors—to give the surface a needed liveliness. Campus architecture should teach as well as house. This one offers a head-scratching lesson in the fugitive nature of appearances.

The South Building introduces a gigantic architectural scale to the campus. Fortunately, it is mainly visible only from Walden Street, so it overwhelms neither campus nor town. It represents the intrusion of big-city, corporate modernism into the rural enclave of Billsville, where the architectural language of giant American corporations has almost never made inroads before. Providing first-rate, flexible laboratory space to attract distinguished scientists to teach at Williams and providing students with first-rate lab spaces where they can learn science by doing it are both admirable ends. The pity is that these ends have been accomplished by visually unsympathetic means. The North Building that replaces Bronfman, by different members of the same firm, makes a striking contrast that bears careful consideration.

11 **Ursula von Rydingsvard, *Large Bowl*, 1997, cast bronze**
Williams College Museum of Art, purchased through the generosity of Alicia V. and Peter B. Pond, Class of 1967

ENDNOTES

1 Perry, 1899, 181–98, is the main source of information about the early history of West College. He lived in the building as an undergraduate in the 1840s, before the interior was rebuilt in the following decade, and so he knew West in its first and second incarnations. He died in 1905, just as the building was undergoing a second major renovation. See "Introduction," note 1.

2 Whitney S. Stoddard, *Reflections on the Architecture of Williams College* (Williamstown, MA: Williams College, 2001), 22–23.

3 "Williams College Alumni," *Boston Post*, January 23, 1891, 5.

4 Minutes of Williams College Trustees Meeting, April 1965.

5 Stoddard, 129.

6 "Architectural Criticism," *Architecture*, August 15, 1909, 113–14.

Spring Street

12   Morgan Hall
J. C. Cady, 1882–83

Long before it opened, Morgan Hall was the sensation of Williams College. To students who only knew dormitories as prim brick crates, like West, East, and South, the playful forms and curvilinear gables of Morgan were utterly baffling. It was the first building on the campus that seemed to be enjoying itself. All through 1882 its construction was followed closely in the pages of the *Argo*, the college's cheeky student magazine. One week it noticed that twenty-four stonecutters were extracting the limestone from Mr. Bullock's quarry; another that seven different nations were represented among the laborers. Certain aspects of Morgan met with the *Argo*'s approval, such as its central heating, which freed space previously taken up by stoves and coal closets. Other aspects distressed it, such as the hyperactive roofline that looked like "a cross between the Star Spangled Banner and the capitol at Albany."[1]

Morgan Hall was the gift of Edwin D. Morgan, governor of New York and later a senator. He did not attend Williams College, but in 1867 he received an honorary degree, and in 1882 he returned the favor with a gift of $100,000 to build a new dormitory. Fortunately, and unusually, the gift came with an architect of the first rank: J. C. Cady, architect of the American Museum of Natural History and the original Metropolitan Opera House. Cady was adept at responding to local conditions and materials, and he quickly decided that the new dormitory would be "essentially old English, with picturesque gables and outline, the material being the light cream colored Williamstown limestone, trimmed with Kentucky limestone." In truth, those picturesque gables were less English than Dutch, a reminder that Williams College is not too far removed from the vigorous Dutch culture of the Hudson River.

Cady, for all his extravagant originality, was a subtle designer. He took into account the sloping site, which can make a building appear to sag, especially if it is symmetrical. To compensate, he anchored the east end with a mighty chimney, giving it a triumphant lift just where it would appear to droop. A few other careful adjustments around the central gable further enhance the sense of dynamic equilibrium. The visitor should walk around the entire building to appreciate Cady's use of stone and how he shifts from carefully squared blocks of rock-faced ashlar on the north to the rubble construction of the south facade.

So successful was Morgan that Marianna Griswold van Rensselaer, America's foremost critic of architecture, praised it in the *Century Magazine* in 1884 as "well composed, expressive, straightforward, dignified, and yet not devoid of picturesqueness…an example to set beside the confused, restless, inorganic structures" of similar eclectic architecture. It is easy to see why the college was eager to summon Cady back three years later to design

Lasell Gymnasium across the street. The gateway they form to Spring Street represents the best of Victorian architecture at Williams, a relaxed, whimsical ensemble that is also sturdy and hardy, and charged with local geology and regional culture. It defies belief that Cady was not summoned back a third time to design Hopkins Hall and complete the architectural trifecta.

Governor Morgan told Cady that anything left over from his $100,000 should be applied to a fund to maintain the dormitory. Both architect and clients were satisfied that the building came in at $80,000, leaving the balance as an endowment for Morgan.

For all its beauty and novelty, Morgan had a disruptive effect on the harmony of the campus. The newest and most luxurious dormitory, it charged the highest rent, and for a time it looked as if the most desirable rooms would be auctioned off to the highest bidder. This amused the impertinent *Argo*, which imagined the Williams of the near future when Morgan would be inhabited only by snobbish millionaires who looked down on their less fortunate peers: "You know, he was a beastly low cad; never roomed in Morgan Hall once, and spent most of his life on the top story of West College. Howwible, aw!"[2] This was not mere fantasy. The seventy students who lived in Morgan represented one-quarter of the student population, but they were the only ones with central heating, indoor plumbing, and bathtubs. Inevitably, their friends would be invited to share the wealth, which soon came to the attention of President Franklin Carter, and with predictable consequences. In December 1883 the *Argo* reported that "the janitor of Morgan has received orders from the President to allow only the occupants of rooms in the Hall the privilege of the bathrooms."[3]

13 Lasell Gymnasium
J. C. Cady, 1885–86

After a twenty-year comedy of errors in gym building, it was nearly miraculous that Williams College could suddenly build as superb a building as Lasell Gymnasium. The first purpose-built gymnasium was old Goodrich Hall (1864), which stood on the site of what is now Thompson Chapel. It was a neo-Gothic mongrel with a bizarre program: a gymnasium at the top, a bowling alley at the bottom, and a chemistry laboratory in between. Goodrich had a multitude of tasks and performed none of them very well. In 1880 an anonymous donor gave President Paul Chadbourne funds to build "a handsome new gymnasium for heavy gymnastics." This latest structure was placed downhill from West College, roughly where the Thompson laboratories now are. It was of wood and looked like a temporary building, which is what it turned out to be. A windstorm destroyed it during the summer of 1883, just as it was about to house the fiftieth reunion dinner for the Class of 1833.

Within weeks of the catastrophe General Benjamin F. Butler, the former governor of Massachusetts, personally donated $5,000 toward the building of a new gym. His example inspired others, but the trustees would not approve the new building until January 1885, by the time they had raised $50,000 in hand. (In fact, it would cost $60,000.) Most of the money came from the Lasell family: the widow of Josiah Lasell (Class of 1844) and his son, Josiah Manning Lasell (Class of 1886). Frederick Ferris Thompson gave the final $1,000 to pay for the great clock in the tower, the first of his many substantial gifts.

Money in hand, President Carter made what is surely the most inspired architectural decision of any Williams president. Rather than interview architects for the new gymnasium or conduct a competition, he simply handed the project over to Cady. The success of his Morgan Hall had made him wildly popular with the administration, trustees, and students, among whom Josiah Lasell numbered

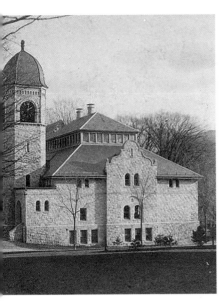 

The great monitor that once crowned the roof of Lasell Gymnasium, necessary when electric lighting was still in its infancy, was removed and replaced with a simple gable when it was remodeled.

at the time. Cady was given the commission and rose to the occasion. He made Lasell a brilliant pendant to Morgan, reprising the same white limestone construction and picturesquely swinging gables, so that the buildings face each other almost as pylons at the top of Spring Street. In their hearty construction, generous suggestion of shelter and warmth, and geological appeal to the Berkshire Mountains, they evoke the character and place of Williams College as splendidly as any buildings ever have.

Before settling on the plans, President Carter visited the recently built gyms at Amherst and Harvard in spring of 1885. The new Williams gym would be up-to-date in every respect, although its equipment sounds quaint to our ears:

> Pulley-weights of the best pattern, adjustable to varying strength, light Indian clubs, dumb-bells, both of wood and of iron, horizontal and parallel bars, rings, and apparatus for developing special muscles, are used under the immediate supervision of an instructor. An inclined running track 229 feet in length, bowling alleys, tub, shower and sponge baths and a baseball court, are important features of the building. There are several class drills daily in the main hall at hours suiting the convenience of the students.[4]

Basketball, which was not invented until 1891, would require further modifications. A new swimming pool was added in 1906, in a wing that carefully followed the style of the original building.

Lasell may have been informed by the Amherst gymnasium, but in one key respect it departed from its neighbor. Amherst practiced a "strict routine… where the student is kept at work exercising in class squads from the time of his entrance until his final exit from the college." At Williams, only freshmen were required to put in three afternoons a week of drill work, and only then until Easter recess. After that they were never again required to enter the building. It was because of just this lack of compulsion that one Williams observer noted with satisfaction, "The Williams gymnasium is filled every day."

14 Lasell Gymnasium Additions
Densmore & Le Clear, 1927; Shreve Lamb & Harmon (squash courts), 1937

The 1920s brought a great surge of public interest in college athletics, which was expressed at Williams in a push to replace Lasell, then almost forty years old, with an entirely new gymnasium. In the fall of 1921 the trustees pledged to raise $400,000 to build a gym with a swimming pool, two basketball courts, seven squash courts, two tennis courts, an indoor running track, and an infield for baseball practice—all in a single multipurpose building. It would have been enormous, far too large for Spring Street, and it was proposed to site it on Cole Field. Before proceeding, President Garfield spoke to the one architect in whom he had absolute confidence: his brother Abram, in Cleveland. On the basis of Abram's sketches, Garfield gave the commission to a Boston firm, Densmore & Le Clear, which submitted preliminary plans in April 1922. (See p. 184.)

President Garfield was a seasoned patron, and he knew all too well how architectural discussions could degenerate into bickering over style, and so he gave his architects an unusual request. They were to avoid showing the elevation drawings to anyone so that discussion would be centered on function and avoid the thorny issues of style and character. Densmore & Le Clear's plan in hand, Garfield asked the trustees to raise enough money to build the gym, hire a professor of athletics, and create an endowment to support athletics— an amount he calculated at $1.5 million. It was a bold request. At a time when many colleges were beginning to worry about an excessive stress on athletics, achieved at the expense of academics, Garfield went against the grain, insisting that "mental perfection cannot be achieved in a body not trained to manual dexterity."[5]

The $1.5 million that Garfield requested was slow in coming, and by 1924 he began to think that it might be better to remain on Spring Street. "What about a one-story, skylighted group of simple brick and tile structures on the old campus, containing nothing but basket-ball and squash courts?" So he wrote to Bentley Warren, the head of the trustees' building committee. But it is often easier to raise money for something audacious than for something

drab and cheap, and Garfield clung to his hope of a vast gym on Cole Field. With his limited resources, he built what he could, beginning with the Cole Field House. (See Walk Four, p. 183.) He held out hope until late 1926, when he threw in the towel. Densmore & Le Clear were instructed to abandon the Cole Field project and instead design a more modest extension to Lasell, "keeping the lines of the present building and the same gray stone." To keep costs down, the firm eliminated the tennis courts and baseball diamond (and, after the first estimates came in, the squash courts), but arranged the plan so that these could be accommodated in a future addition.

The builder was J. R. Hampson Co., of Pittsfield, supervised by the college's superintendent of buildings and grounds, Perry Smedley. Excavation began in late 1926 and involved a good deal of blasting of bedrock. Fortunately, the stone matched the original material of Lasell, and where possible, it was incorporated into the new building. So closely do they match, in fact, that most observers cannot distinguish the 1886 building from its 1927 sibling. It is unclear how much of this scrupulous response to the historic character of the campus is due to Ralph Adams Cram, who knew the campus extremely well and whose firm served as consulting architect to Densmore & Le Clear.

It would take another decade to add the squash courts, although this happened in a roundabout way. In early 1936, trustee Quincy Bent (Class of 1901), vice president of Bethlehem Steel, was appointed head of the college's executive committee on building improvements. There was considerable pressure from alumni to build a new hockey rink and baseball batting cage, particularly since Amherst and Wesleyan had recently built similar facilities. An estimate was secured from Frick & Co., the builders of the hockey rink at West Point. The much-needed squash courts could be squeezed into the "small outmoded structure" that housed the present batting cage (this was a utilitarian shed on the athletic field). The college's new president, Tyler Dennett, cautiously endorsed the project: his principal mission, he said, was to enhance and support faculty and curriculum but that "adequate athletic facilities are part of the college's improvement plan."

At some point between March 1936 and the following November, the trustees decided that squash was more important than hockey. The reason is unclear, but it may simply have been that the trustees found it easier to raise money for squash courts among wealthy alumni (after all, in New York there is the Racquet Club on Park Avenue and no similar hockey establishment). Bent and two other trustees combined to contribute the $100,000 for fourteen single squash courts and one doubles squash court. To keep costs down, no showers were to be added; Lasell with its showers was close enough.

Rather than build the extension that Densmore & Le Clear had proposed, a new freestanding building was erected. The designer was William Frederick Lamb (Class of 1904), of Shreve Lamb & Harmon, who had designed the Empire State Building (for which the college awarded him an honorary degree in 1932). The building opened in January 1938, although some of the courts were not yet finished; each of the carefully smoothed plaster interiors required five days of work by two men. It was still new the following year when a recently hired assistant professor of art, S. Lane Faison Jr. (Class of 1929), wrote a lengthy letter to the *North Adams Transcript*, taking the recent buildings of the college to task. Squash courts were a modern phenomenon and deserved a modern expression; they should not be shoehorned "into the semblance of Griffin hall." Faison's attack against "phony Georgian" was the first salvo in an architectural crusade that eventually brought a modern building to the Williams campus, but not until two more decades passed.

15   Simon Squash Center
Michael Wurmfeld Associates, 1998

The decision to bring the squash courts at American colleges into conformity with international standards required enlarging the ones in the 1938 building, and the growing popularity of the game at Williams necessitated building new ones as well. An architect and squash player, Michael Wurmfeld, was chosen by the squash coach, Dave Johnson (Class of 1971), to design the courts. Wurmfeld played at the McKim, Mead & White Racquet Club on Park Avenue, New York City, where Johnson had been the pro in residence, but they did not meet there. Johnson inquired at Princeton about a possible architect; Wurmfeld was recommended. The result is a happy blend of form and function. Despite the skepticism of the director of Buildings and Grounds, Wurmfeld was able to fit new courts inside the Shreve, Lamb and Harmon walls, with inches to spare. An amazing team of Italian plasterers was imported to make the walls of the new courts.

Wurmfeld's addition, with its angled entrance under a deep cantilever, gives the building a commanding presence in the open space enclosed by the south side of Lawrence Hall and the north and east sides of the Chandler Athletic facility, even though the Wurmfeld addition is smaller than its neighbors. He designed a vivid sunburst pavement radiating out from the door of his squash courts to enliven and organize the entire open space, but that was seen as visually too exciting for Williamstown. A conservative geometric design of no excitement whatsoever took its place.

16 Chandler Athletic Complex
Cambridge Seven Associates, 1987

A sprawling collection of brick rectangles, the Chandler Athletic Complex contains at its east end the college swimming pool, from which winning teams surface almost annually. The entrance, at right angles to the pool, is frequently closed for reasons of security, as is the entrance to the squash courts. Inside are offices for coaches on the upper floor and a basketball court, partly visible through glass inserted into the north wall, around the corner that one passes on the way to or from Spring Street, where the commercial extension of Chandler terminates in a tower. A bridge connects the complex with the labyrinthine interiors of the older gym and the squash courts. Although the decorative touches of Williams purple can seem excessive, the building offers a major gift to the community in the wide, triangular plaza formed by the north side of the pool and the entrance wall to the west. A wall of glass on the south side allows easy viewing of the team's practice sessions in the fifty-meter Olympic pool, which can be divided into two twenty-five-yard sections when necessary. Swimmers doing the backstroke can admire the way the roof truss is integrated with the ventilation system, the air outtakes

spaced precisely between each truss, the pipes expanding as they converge on the outlet. Outside, under the pavement of the plaza, are the water pumping systems for the pool. Covering them brought about a rise in ground level that created the plaza and cut off the staircase that once led up to Charles Moore's "ironic" Ionic columns on the north side of the plaza. (See Walk Three, p. 122.) This may be almost the only "urban" space on campus.

17　Lansing Chapman Hockey Rink
Mollenburg and Betz, 1953, 1961, 1969

Hockey, a sport with a long history in what used to be much colder New England winters, finally got an artificial rink (usable in above-freezing

temperatures) in 1953. But it had only rink boards and ice, and when the wind blew the right way, the nearby coal pile covered the ice with little black specks. Eight years later a round-arched, vaulted roof, pure in shape and clear in structure, was raised over the ice, but the ends were left open, so the rink became a wind tunnel. Another eight years on, the ends were enclosed, much to the relief of both the players and the fans. This history demonstrates that athletics do not always dominate the architectural culture of Williams, even though they have a prominent place. During the off season, indoor tennis courts are installed in the rink.

18   Herbert Towne Field House
Lockwood Greene, 1970

Enormous laminated wooden arches support vaults that soar over the vast interior (the largest enclosed space on campus), designed for indoor exercise in frigid Williamstown winters. The arches spring from massive concrete buttresses that enliven the exterior. Every now and again the field house hosts huge parties thrown by the administration for the faculty and staff. In bad weather, townsfolk, faculty, and students alike walk inside for their health.

19   Gargoyle Gate
Squires & Wynkoop, 1906

> The French Gothic character of the building…was suggested by the fact
> that the society itself took its name from the Gothic gargoyles on one of
> the dormitories of the college.
> —Frederick A. Squires (*Arts & Decoration*, 1911)

When old Goodrich Hall was demolished in 1902, someone had the bright idea
to salvage the limestone blocks and incorporate them in "the construction
of a gargoyle gate to the Weston athletic field." It took several years for the
Gargoyle Society to raise the money and procure plans. It seems that one
of the gargoyles, Walter Squires (Class of 1904), recommended his elder
brother, Frederick A. Squires (Class of 1900), a promising architect who had
just opened his practice. The result is a modest gem by an architect with an
uncommonly deep understanding of the problem and the site.

The entrance to Weston Field was originally marked by this gate in the rustic style of an
Adirondack camp. By 1902 it was old-fashioned, and Olmsted Brothers recommended replacing it
with something that would give "architectural emphasis" to the field. This challenge was seized by
the Gargoyle Society, which had been founded in 1895 to "take active steps for the advancement
of Williams in every branch of college life and work." The Gargoyle Gate remains the society's most
conspicuous contribution to the college.

Previously, the athletic field had been entered through a simple rustic gate, pedestrians and carriages crowding through together in a confused mass. Frederick Squires's first task was to separate the two streams of traffic, which he did by creating a round ticket booth with windows on both sides. Pedestrians entered through the low sheltering arch, while carriages passed on the outside. It would have been easy to put the ticket booth in the center, making a symmetrical composition, but Squires decided that this would yield a "weak and uninteresting building."[6] Instead, he explained, the goal was balance rather than symmetry.

Squires was particularly concerned with scale and whether his small object would hold its own in its vast setting.

> Small as the gateway is the question of the form was important. The surroundings are impressive, with a great circle of Berkshire Hills surrounding the field and Mt. Greylock in the distance. It required a sturdy building to hold its own where the natural surroundings were on so great a scale. Nothing would have been a greater mistake than to have had iron gates and posts.[7]

Squires's answer was a composition whose parts were few and simple: a tough cylindrical tower, a low conical roof, and a broad entrance arch whose lift is like the flexing of one long and mighty muscle. (He made sure to keep the arch so low that impetuous carriage drivers would not be able to pass under it.)

Over the decades, more than half a dozen alumni returned to design buildings for Williams College, but none took as much sheer evident pleasure from working with the Berkshire landscape. In only one respect was Squires disappointed. In 1911, five years after its completion, he promised that "gargoyles are to be carved out of the rough corbels supporting the wooden arch of the gate, which will serve to give extra prominence to the society which erected it." More than a century later, the Gargoyle Gate is still awaiting its gargoyles.

In its original form, the Gargoyle Society was a self-perpetuating group of leading members of the senior class who elected their successors from the junior class every spring. Election to Gargoyle was a signal achievement for an undergraduate. In the 1960s a waggish group of students created a counter organization, Gurgle. They invented a trophy awarded to the hardest-drinking member of the senior class. Annually, seniors elect the member of their class who has accomplished the most for the college as winner of the Grosvenor Cup. The winner of the Gurgle trophy gloried in the award of the Grosswinner's Cup, a toilet bowl. With time, Gurgle went down the drain.

20   Weston Field Athletic Complex
Clough, Harbor Associates, 2014

Weston Field, for many decades the site of a football field bereft of almost every convenience save ample space for tailgating, sported a decrepit grandstand for the home folks and even worse for visitors. Visiting teams had to retire to the distant Field House at halftime, and for many years women spectators were offered no handy restrooms at all.

That changed with the erection of the new grandstand and press box, with restrooms and concession stands below the sturdy bleachers that hold 1,400 fans. Visiting teams now have a locker room inside the new structure at the south

end of the field, as do their coaches. And of course there are ample locker room spaces for all the male and female teams that play on the field. Clough, Harbor Associates—mainly an engineering firm—designed both the buildings and the entire site.

The football field thriftily doubles as a lacrosse field in the spring. Women's field hockey now has its own playing space, south of the new building and surrounded by a well-constructed running track, which, unlike the former track, is up to NCAA standards. Overlooking the field hockey area is an ancient stand, once built for watching baseball games, moved to its present site and renamed in honor of Bob Peck, a former director of athletics. The football/lacrosse area, Farley-Lamb Field, bears the names of two very successful coaches.

From all reports, the Athletics Department is extremely happy with its new, upgraded accommodations. Although function has been well served, the visuals are disappointing for a project that came in at $22 million and change. The concrete-block exteriors of the building at the south end of the football field are something of an embarrassment, while the interiors remind one of cheap motels.

21   B&L Building
Burr and McCallum, 2011–12

To replace a service station, B&L Gulf, that stood on the northeast corner of Spring and Latham Streets, Andy Burr (Class of 1966) and his wife and partner, Ann McCallum, designed the multiuse facility that retains the name of the very busy filling station that once served a good part of the Williamstown community. One could drop off a car for an oil change, walk to work, and then pick it up on the way home. Before the internet, this was typically where faculty first learned who had just been tenured. That was one of the conveniences that Spring Street once offered to make Williamstown a pedestrian community, even for those who had to drive to work. On the street, at one time, were a grocery store, a drugstore, a magazine and newspaper store, and as many as two bookstores. At least the post office still remains, and a bookstore that also sells magazines and newspapers is now again in place. A pharmacy and grocery are likely never to return.

The B&L building is a witty comment on the traditional commercial architecture of Spring Street. The dark red relates to the older brick buildings, even though the metal siding is different, to recall the industrial architecture of New England that the architects admire. The scale of the windows picks up the scale typical of the structures along the street. A metal "cornice" plays with the variations on the theme of cornice in which many of the buildings to the north indulge.

At its north end, the B&L steps back from the sidewalk to create a little breathing space and to make room for an entrance into the apartments and the college's Human Resources offices on the upper level. Anchoring the corner at

sidewalk level is one of the most popular student hangouts in town, Tunnel City Coffee, thronged most of the day and into the evening by students sitting at tables, working on computers. In summer, the garage doors that form parts of the cafe walls can be rolled up to open the interior to the street. The doors are reminiscent of McCallum's native Montreal, where cafes often open to the sidewalk in good weather. The B&L offers an object lesson in how to make a building that fits into its environment without being derivative, sentimental, or boring.

22   Williams Inn
Cambridge Seven Associates, 2016–19

To replace the tired and architecturally dreadful Williams Inn that stood across from Field Park (it was designed by an architect who specialized in bowling alleys), the college erected a new inn at the foot of Spring Street. This building (Stefanie Greenfield, principal designer) not only upgrades the facility itself but also contributes a needed boost to commercial traffic on the only shopping street in town.

Greenfield's concept of the building derived from the type of New England farmhouse complex that once might have stood on the site, back when Williamstown was a village of farmers. The main house, of stone, is the main entrance to the inn, even though it modestly turns its front to the west to avoid a deliberate attempt to dominate the street. The far simpler barn, sheathed in wood, stands behind and to the east of the main house; it contains a restaurant, marked by a wide glass wall. The third part, the back house, runs south from the main house to provide the lion's share of the rooms. The rather irregular L of the plan reflects the fact that the building is restricted to the only part of the site that is legally buildable. The inn stands on a sort of island, surrounded by wetlands, which can be crossed on a footbridge that connects the end of Spring Street to the restaurant. Cars cross a larger bridge on a winding road that leads to the Main House. The inn was still in the design phase at the time of this writing.

23 Susan B. Hopkins House
Architect unknown, ca. 1920

When Mary Hopkins, the widow of Mark Hopkins, died in 1898, she left the bulk of her estate to her unmarried daughter, Susan B. Hopkins, with one attention-getting proviso: if Susan ever married, she would have to share the estate equally with six other beneficiaries. She never married, and she worked to preserve the Hopkins family legacy, as in 1927, when she consulted on the form of the Hopkins Memorial Gate. She died in 1944, the last of Mark Hopkins's eight children, and passed her estate to her nephew Henry Hopkins Jr., no strings attached. The college acquired the house in 1969.

Susie Hopkins, as it is lovingly called, is a shingled bungalow in a Dutch Colonial vein. The bold chimneys, ample dormers, and characteristic gambrel roof—to maximize the amount of usable space in the attic—strike a homey note. But its best feature is the relaxed and informal way it sits harmoniously on its wooded site. Its architect is unknown, but it may well have been H. Neill Wilson,

a prolific Pittsfield architect who designed similar gambrel-roofed cottages in and around Williamstown.

24   Oakley Center for the Humanities and Social Sciences, formerly Makepeace House
Harding & Seaver (?), ca. 1915–25

What is today known as the Oakley Center was for years the house of Charles D. Makepeace, who graduated from Williams in 1900. Although his "family has long been involved in the cranberry canning industry," as articles about him invariably mentioned, he came to realize that he was more interested in Williams than cranberries, and he left the family business to return as college treasurer in 1935. When he died in 1960, the bulk of his estate went to the college, and eventually his house did as well.

Since 1985 the house has served as the Oakley Center, providing offices for faculty on leave and colloquia and conferences for faculty, staff, and students. It is purely a coincidence, although a pleasant one, that this humane initiative takes place in a house called Makepeace. *Nomen omen.*

25 The Log

Kenneth Reynolds, 1941 and later; Restoration: C&H Architects, 2015

Inside the Log, a repurposed and expanded house, the wood-paneled interiors designed by Kenneth Reynolds (Class of 1916) produce a cozy environment enlivened by large murals that tell stories about the college's early history. One,

TOP **The Log, interior** BOTTOM **Stanley Rowland, "Ephraim Williams and Chief Hendrick Planning the Battle of Lake George,"1942**

in the front room, that depicts a moment of planning before the Battle of Lake George by Ephraim Williams and his Native American ally, the Mohawk chief known as Hendrick, caused something of an uproar in 2015, when a student objected to the way Native Americans are portrayed. A text posted next to the painting explains the controversy and puts it into historical context. From an artistic point of view, the work exemplifies the way American muralists of the 1930s and 1940s based their work in good part on mural painters of the Italian Renaissance. For instance, the pose of the figure of Williams in his red coat apes that of John the Baptist in Piero della Francesca's *Baptism of Christ* in the National Gallery, London, as do the arching shapes of the trees imitate Piero's.

The Log, originally intended for alumni returning for athletic events, has now become a beautifully refurbished and much-frequented restaurant serving the whole community at lunch and dinner under Reynolds's heroically scaled wooden beams.

26 Williams Bookstore
Cambridge Seven Associates, 2015–17

Occupying the northwest corner of Spring and Walden Streets, the new bookstore (Stefanie Greenfield, principal designer) marks the end of the

Williams Bookstore, interior of cafe

commercial row on the west side of Spring with a strong corner, recessed to provide pedestrian breathing room at the entrance. Three stories in height, the building offers trade sales and a cafe at ground level, textbooks and college memorabilia on the second level, and rental office space on top. The last is reached by a separate entrance on Walden Street. Topping it all off is an array of floating solar panels, a sign of the college's commitment to environmental sensitivity. The exterior—brick, cedar, and glass—is marked by a syncopated rhythm of openings in the wall that brings a contemporary beat to the commercial architecture of the street, while continuing its tradition of brick architecture. Remarkable is the consonance of the orange/brown cedar siding with the orange/brown brick of the commercial buildings just to the north on the same side of the street.

The interior is delightfully surprising. The intimate cafe snuggles under a curved wooden ceiling that continues without interruption down the wall to form the bench on which customers sit in a sophisticated espresso cave. On the other side of the bench wall, behind the sales desk, similar wooden paneling rises two floors to curve across to the front wall. Although the interior is hardly huge, skillful use of transparent, reflective glass opens it into a Cubist fantasy.

Returning a bookstore to Spring Street, from which it had been absent for decades, is part of an effort to rejuvenate the town's commercial heart, which has suffered from the competition of lower prices offered by national chains.

In summer, there is a pleasant outdoor cafe, with a serpentine bench under umbrellas, on the Walden Street side.

ENDNOTES

1 "College Notes," *Argo*, September 30, 1882, 94.

2 "What May Be Expected," *Argo,* March 24, 1883, 234.

3 "College Notes," *Argo,* December 15, 1885, 167.

4 *Catalogue of Williams College, 1902–1903* (Williamstown, MA: Williams College, 1902), 63.

5 "College Chief Approves Sports," *Binghamton Press and Sun-Bulletin,* April 10, 1922, 15.

6 Frederick A. Squires, "The Gargoyle Gate," *Arts & Decoration,* January 1911, 130.

7 Ibid.

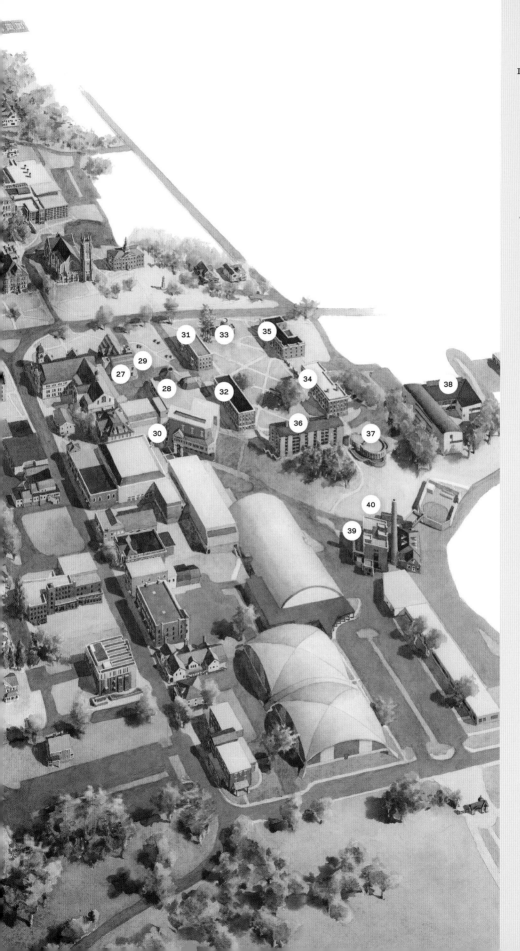

27   Goodrich Hall

Gervase Wheeler, 1858–59; Conversion to library: Harding & Seaver, 1906–7, 1915; Conversion to snack bar: Bruner/Cott Associates, 1997; Facade stabilization: Christopher Williams Architects, 2017–18

For a calm, gently understated Gothic chapel, Goodrich Hall is bursting with volatile ideas about architecture, religion, and symbolism. When students initially learned in 1857 that the college planned to build its first freestanding chapel, they wondered "whether another of these long rectangular objects is to find its way among our shades, to blur the eyes of coming generations, or whether a structure of Gothic proportions is to ornament our College grounds."[1]

They need not have worried. The college chose an ardent champion of the Gothic Revival for its architect, Gervase Wheeler, an English émigré. Instead of the "long rectangular object" feared by students, Wheeler delivered a gleefully irregular composition of sprawling high-gabled volumes, pinned together by the lofty spiky tower to the side (long since decapitated). His materials were equally picturesque: rubble walls of dolomite, from a quarry two miles to the west on Route 2, and a mighty open roof truss within of oiled chestnut. Two local builders, Samuel Keyes of Bennington and Monroe Temple of Adams, laid the foundations in early 1858; the building was dedicated at commencement the following year. It could easily have been a parish church in rural England, which seems to be precisely what the trustees wanted.

The question is, why did they want it? In 1857 Williams was still a sectarian college, officially Congregationalist, and proud of its Puritan roots. According to those roots, Congregationalists did not build churches but meetinghouses—auditorium-like spaces with clear lines of sight and sound— with nothing suggestive of mystery and symbolism. And yet Goodrich looks like a High Church Anglican chapel that has gotten confused and wandered onto a Calvinist campus.

This is not to say that the college aspired to Anglicanism (President Mark Hopkins once quipped that an Episcopalian is little better than a Catholic). And in fact, Wheeler carefully adjusted his Anglican model to fit Congregationalist worship. There was no altar but merely a raised platform with a plain desk for the officiating preacher. Nor was there a single processional aisle but one to either side, as in an auditorium, as the two entrances imply. Wheeler delivered an imaginative hybrid that balanced tradition and fashionability, a Puritan plan in a Gothic Revival skin.

The reason for that adroit balancing act is easy to find. Harvard had just built itself a prestigious new chapel in the strikingly modern architectural style known as the *Rundbogenstil*, the synthetic round-arched style devised in progressive German architectural circles. Such a statement of architectural modernity suited Harvard's theological modernity. In the early nineteenth

Gervase Wheeler brought from his native England the idea that churches in remote and rural regions should be built in a hardy, less-developed style. Hence the Early English Gothic mode of Goodrich Hall, with its simple lancet windows and broad passages of rugged stone walls.

Congregationalist meetinghouses scrupulously avoided the central aisle of Catholic churches, which implied movement toward a holy altar in a chancel at the east end. Here there is no processional movement, only a space of communal gathering.

century Harvard had become Unitarian, the progressive wing of Puritanism that stressed reason over faith. Unitarians rejected the Trinitarianism of orthodox Puritans—who believed in a Holy Trinity of Father, Son, and Holy Ghost—and instead believed in a single God ("at most," as the rude joke goes).

Today this might seem a doctrinal trifle, but for Williams in the 1850s it was a matter of truth against heresy. And so while Harvard placed a brilliant window above its pulpit, as a symbol of reason and enlightenment, Williams placed there a defiant symbol of the Trinity. This is the medieval symbol known as the *Scutum Fidei*, a shield with the Latin abbreviations for the Trinity, which still survives in a forlorn fragment in the apex of the south wall. It requires an act of imagination to appreciate how serious this battle of symbols was, when plucky Williams raised itself up to shout scorn at what it felt was a nest of skeptics and heretics at the other end of Massachusetts.

But as the college was performing a tricky balancing act with its chapel, it did not want to steer so clear of pure reason that it backed into the realm of mysticism. President Hopkins took care to reassure the college in his dedication that there was no taint of idolatry in building a beautiful chapel: "We do not think of architecture as a means, or direct aid of worship; nor of the spirit of beauty as the Spirit of God." One should think of architectural beauty as the expression of an intellectual idea and not a devotional act. As for the architectural form of the chapel,

> its parts have a relation that may be said to symbolize, not inaptly, the proper relation of ideas and ends in a College. In front, prominent and beautiful, is the Chapel, which represents the great ideas of religious instruction and worship. Separate from this, yet connected by the tower and spire, heaven-ward pointing for both, are the rooms for the instruction of the two upper classes; and over these, united with each and all, is the Alumni Hall. So, through worship and instruction, religious and secular, but both pointing to heaven, would we raise our Alumni to their own place, and send them thence into the world.[2]

President Hopkins may have assigned intellectual meaning to those secular spaces to the rear of his building, but in fact they were an expression of poverty. Since the building of West College, the cash-starved college had invariably crammed multiple functions into its buildings. Even at its dedication there were already complaints that the thirty-two-by-fifty-foot wing to the rear containing the alumni hall was woefully inadequate. So was the chapel itself, although not until 1878 was it enlarged with a broad transept to the west, closely matching the materials and details of the original construction.

As the first stone building (after the Hopkins Observatory) on the all-brick campus, the chapel brought about a revolution in the college's architecture, and until the end of the century dolomite was the material of choice for monumental buildings. As late as 1902 the Olmsted brothers recommended that the college "adhere to the local bluish white limestone as the exterior building material for all future buildings." And it is quite likely that it would have, had not a sudden enthusiasm for colonial architecture set in.

When Thompson Chapel was completed in 1905, Goodrich was freed from religious duty, which was marked by the removal of its spire. It was converted to serve as a reading room for adjacent Lawrence Hall, then still functioning as a library. Since then, it has served variously as a lecture hall, painting and print studios, and now a student center and coffee shop. It should be pointed out that the building did not get its name until the original Goodrich, an exercise hall on the site of Thompson Chapel, was demolished in 1903.

28   Lawrence Hall

Thomas Tefft, 1846–47; Francis R. Allen, 1890; Harding & Seaver, 1917, 1926, 1938; Charles Moore of Moore Grover Harper, 1977–83, 1984–86

It took seven distinct building campaigns, spread over a century and a half, to create the sprawling architectural jamboree known as Lawrence Hall. Architects major and minor added to it—in 1890, 1917, 1926, 1938, 1982, and 1986—until what had once been a compact and freestanding octagon was nearly swallowed up by its additions. But even engulfed within a much larger whole, it commands attention. And deservedly so: it is the single most consequential building of Williams College and, in fact, the only one of national significance.

Buildings can be innovative in their plan or their style, and Lawrence Hall is extraordinary in both. The plan was the creation of Charles Coffin Jewett, the brilliant librarian of Brown University (and friend of the donor, Amos Lawrence). Jewett recommended that Williams adopt a radical new plan on the panopticon principle, consisting of a central hub from which stacks of books radiate outward. Such a plan had been used for prison architecture but not yet for a library. Taking as his model an unbuilt proposal for a panopticon library in Paris, Jewett reduced it to a little jewel box of a building just forty-eight feet across and forty feet high. The library itself was upstairs, in a domed rotunda (once lighted by a glazed oculus) carried on eight Ionic columns. These were copied, line for exquisite line, from the fifth-century BCE. Temple on the Ilissos, as published in the first volume of James Stuart and Nicholas Revett's *Antiquities of Athens* (1762). Behind each column were to be cast-iron bookshelves that ran to the outer walls, creating seven book alcoves (the eighth compartment was reserved for the staircase), each with a generous round-arched window; the librarian sitting at the central desk could monitor all of them. The library was to be internally expandable, with three sets of shelves stacked on top of each other, but the proposed gallery and iron bookcases were never installed.

FROM LEFT **East College, Fayerweather, Lawrence Hall; foreground, Louise Bourgeois,** *Eyes,* **2001**

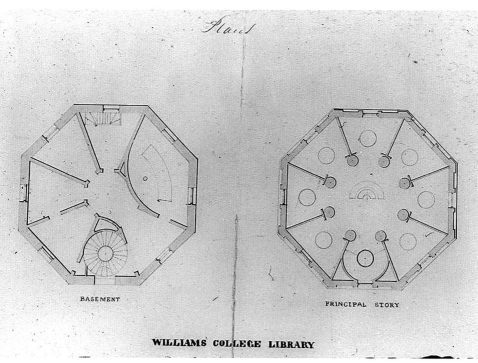

BASEMENT

PRINCIPAL STORY

WILLIAMS COLLEGE LIBRARY

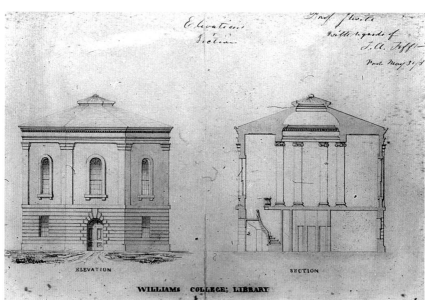

ELEVATION

SECTION

WILLIAMS COLLEGE LIBRARY

Lawrence Hall has been enlarged so many times that it has lost the geometric clarity of its original form, a pristine octagon with light streaming in from windows on all eight sides and from its oculus above.

Rationality and idealism: the panopticon plan, which lets the librarian monitor every alcove from a central desk, is the instrument of modern efficiency, while the Greek columns and Roman dome speak of the ancient dignity of reading and the book.

Jewett also recommended the architect for the new library, his protégé Thomas Tefft, a nineteen-year-old prodigy from Providence, Rhode Island. This marks the first time that Williams availed itself of professional architectural advice. Although Tefft had not yet enrolled at Brown University, where he graduated in 1851, his design for Lawrence Hall was no mere juvenilia. It was a shrewd and imaginative essay in an architectural style that was scarcely known in the United States, the *Rundbogenstil* of contemporary Germany. The round-arched style was defiantly modern; instead of imitating a historical style to evoke nostalgic associations, it derived its forms from the objective expression of the materials and system of construction. The new State Library in Munich (1832–43) gave Tefft his point of departure. He took its system of repeated round arches, outlined in continuous projecting surrounds, and adapted it to a panopticon plan, which he encased in a brick octagon. At Lawrence Hall, French ideas about planning collided with German ideas about style—to produce an octagonal form that would soon be a short-lived fad for American houses. All this and with a pure specimen of Greek Revival archaeology within. Seldom do so many architectural ideas converge so fruitfully and in so small a space.

Tefft's Lawrence Hall should not be confused with a library in the modern sense. In 1846 Williams was essentially a school that specialized in the education of future Congregationalist ministers. Lawrence was not a research library or a recreational library (all fiction was in the collections of the college's various student societies). Nor was there was anything by Rousseau, Spinoza, or that Harvard-taught heretic Ralph Waldo Emerson. As the 1852 catalog shows, its collection was devoted almost exclusively to history and theology. Students did not write research papers, not in the modern sense, and consequently they did not spend much time in the stacks. Nor could they. According to the posted hours, the library was almost never open:

> Senior and Junior Sophisters, shall have the privilege of borrowing and returning books every Wednesday afternoon, and the Sophomores and Freshmen, every Saturday afternoon, in term time.

(As a special favor, the library was also open the first Friday of the semester.) Lawrence Hall was in effect a storage library and little more. But as the college began to widen its scope and offer more science courses, books began to pour in at an increasing rate. By 1888, the original collection of 7,000 books had grown to 19,000; additions were soon added to either side of the octagon and, shortly thereafter, to the south. In 1917 Harding & Seaver drew up plans for yet another expansion to the south, but by now it was clear that the library needs of Williams could not be met by adding an infinite number of wings to Lawrence. Two years later it was determined to build an entirely new library, Stetson Hall, upon whose completion Lawrence was transformed into the college's art museum. The alterations were again designed by Harding & Seaver, who diligently designed further additions throughout the 1930s, only one of which was built (the Blashfield Room, 1938).

The visitor to Lawrence Hall should not leave without inspecting the rotunda, with its gorgeously carved Ionic capitals, arguably the college's finest interior. In particular, one should also note how sensitively the architect Francis Allen related his 1890 wings to the original octagon, enlarging the building even as he deferred to it, a case study in how to add to a building. Finally, the inscription carved in the entrance lintel terminates in a period, a very odd feature in a lapidary text. Was Tefft saying that this was the final word in library design?

*   *   *

When Stetson Hall opened in 1925 as the new college Library, the Art and Classics Departments took over Lawrence Hall. Classics stayed only a few years. The rotunda and its wings became the site for the display for what was then a modest permanent art collection. There were no teaching spaces in the building; the firm of Harding & Seaver provided a two-story T extending from

Lawrence Hall, rotunda

the octagon's south face that branched into three stories at the south end in response to the slope of the site. A new entrance was established at the east wall of the stem of the T. Upstairs in the crossbar of the T was a large lecture hall and a smaller space for temporary exhibitions, while the two lower stories below were designed with two squarish rooms for recitations. Outside, the building was a clean brick box; the thrifty simplicity continued inside.

In the 1930s, as the museum collection grew, additional spaces were added to the west side of the stem of the T. Upstairs was a gallery, named for the nineteenth-century muralist Edwin Howland Blashfield, with a tile floor, rough plaster walls, leaded-glass windows, and wooden ceiling beams that recall the interiors of the Isabella Stewart Gardner Museum in Boston. Below was the commodious Cluett Gallery that housed a collection of Spanish paintings donated by the well-to-do Cluett family from Troy, New York. A group of major works from the Museum of Fine Arts in Boston spent World War II safely in that space. In 1951 the college museum partnered with Bennington College to mount the first retrospective exhibition of the paintings of Jackson Pollock. S. Lane Faison Jr. said he could have bought *Autumn Rhythm*, the great Pollock that now belongs to the Metropolitan Museum, for $5,000. "If I had," he noted ruefully, "I would have been fired."

In 1936 Harding & Seaver prepared a plan to add a second T to the south of their original T to create additional museum and teaching spaces, but no construction followed. President Phinney Baxter, always pressed for money, deliberately kept the Art Department and the museum on a tight economic leash, lest they outgrow their very modest budgets. That situation persisted until Jack Sawyer became president in 1961. Sawyer told Faison that although he wished he could expand every department, finances would allow him to develop only one from each division. From the humanities he chose Art. Even so, the museum's desperate need for more space, better security, and climate control had to wait until the presidency of John Chandler, and then to endure a delay caused by a recession, before the college was prepared to add on to Lawrence once again. A committee headed by Whitney Stoddard, who taught a course called Modern Architecture, picked Charles Moore to design it.

The selection of Moore, then teaching at UCLA, one of the most important and inventive Postmodern architects, was an adventurous move for a college that had traditionally gone with competent professionals rather than architects on the cutting edge, which Postmodernism certainly was in 1977. The design process went through many stages, three museum directors, and the interrupting recession that caused the athletic component to be split off and postponed for financial reasons. When the final project went out to bid, it was way over a budget that had been established without first really considering the museum's needs. The project was trimmed mercilessly. Moore's deliciously whimsical historical trim was scrubbed from the exterior; he paid for the set of Ionic columns in the rear at ground level himself (Stoddard dubbed them the "Ironic Order"). Even so, the atrium that connects the older parts of the building to the Moore addition is the most dynamic space Williams College has ever enjoyed.

Moore's clever solution to the difficulties of the site largely survived. Lawrence Hall is hemmed in by Goodrich to the west, and East and Fayerweather to the east. The lawn to the north is inviolate, because to build on it would forever hide Tefft's elegant octagon. To the south, the land slopes steeply down to a level that was originally two stories below the bottom floor of the 1920s T. The only direction the building could expand was south, off the cliff. Tefft's front door could no longer be used, because it could never provide handicapped access. A legal new entrance had to go on the east side, since the building's west side sidles up to a precipitous ravine that the witty Moore at one point proposed to turn into a slinky version of Rome's Spanish Steps.

The new entrance leads into the two-story atrium that connects old and new. To the right rises the brick south wall of the 1920s T. Soaring overhead is a bridge, a Futurist vision of solid forms thrusting through space. That's the "modern" part of a design whose mannerist "post" parts include Michelangelesque brackets from the Laurentian Library. A wall painted with a

Lawrence Hall, Charles Moore addition, entrance atrium

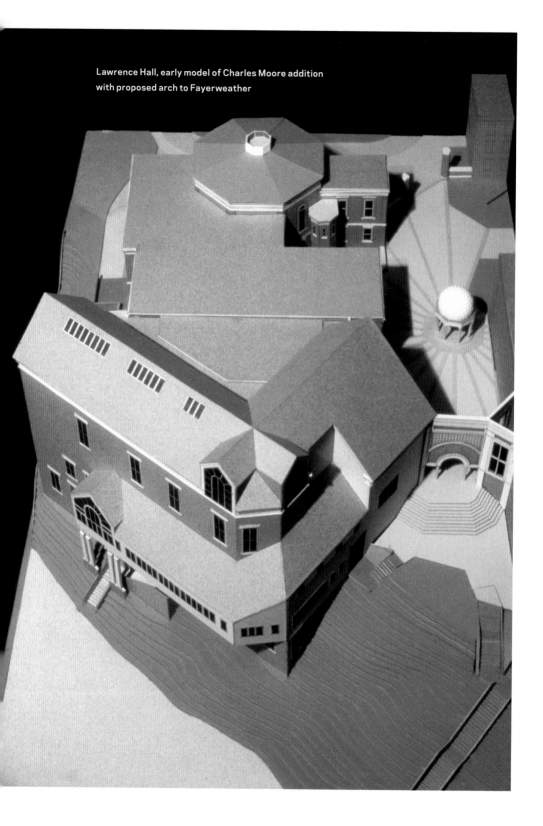

Lawrence Hall, early model of Charles Moore addition
with proposed arch to Fayerweather

Lawrence Hall, Charles Moore addition

design by Sol LeWitt backs up the staircase that first ducks under the bridge and then zips up to the top floor. This staircase offers a telling example of how Moore understood the relation between nature and architecture. At the top of the steps, visitors may note that the enclosing wall of the stair is not quite parallel to the wall with the LeWitt. This is no mistake. The wall with the LeWitt rises from the edge of the cliff that falls away to the south, its location indicating the shape of the land on which it stands. The staircase, on the other hand, is set at a forty-five-degree angle to the bridge that spans the atrium. That bridge is part of the north–south axis that Moore established to fuse the new and old parts of the building. He gloried in revealing the conflict between natural geography and human-imposed geometry. This may be the most interesting architectural detail on the whole campus, as well as one of the easiest to overlook—Moore liked to reward attentive observers.

Increased museum spaces consist, on the upper floor, of two new galleries, a smaller and a larger, set at right angles to each other. The axis of the bridge leads directly into the southeastern end of the larger gallery, whose polygonal walls rhyme with Tefft's original octagon at the northern end of the axis. Moore intended to float an octagonal dome outlined by the glow from concealed light sources over the gallery end, but then came budget cuts.

No sooner had the museum addition opened in 1983 than a chance for another expansion arose. Eugenie Prendergast, widow of the painter Charles Prendergast, the brother of the more famous Maurice Prendergast, offered to give her collection of her late husband's and brother-in-law's paintings, as well as a generous endowment, to the museum. Thomas Krens, then the director, accepted the gift and called on Moore Grover Harper to provide additional space, which they did by designing two superimposed, irregular octagons to fill in the area on the east side of Lawrence between the wings of the 1890s and the 1920s. Mrs. Prendergast did not care for the octagonal gallery at ground level intended for her collection, and so the old lecture hall and old temporary exhibition space in the T, both on the top floor, became the Prendergast Galleries. The museum reopened in 1986 with a retrospective exhibition of Moore's work.

29   Louise Bourgeois, *Eyes*, 2001, bronze, granite, electric light
Williams College Museum of Art, commissioned on the occasion of the museum's seventy-fifth anniversary

At age ninety, Louise Bourgeois created this nine-part suite of eyes on which kids can play and adults bask in the sun. (See pp. 116–17.) Some line a winding path that leads through a voluptuously rolling landscape, a key part of the installation, to the museum. Eyes for Bourgeois were for seeing and for erotic play. Thus her eyes have forms that suggest other body parts. The work is playful, but a bit menacing—all those eyes observing our every move. At night, Bourgeois's eyes light up, perhaps in anticipation of events that take place in the dark.

30   Herbert Ferber, *Calligraph LC*, 1967–68, copper
Williams College Museum of Art, gift of Edith Ferber

Herbert Ferber's lively letters *L* and *C* monumentalize the act of calligraphic writing—that is, the gestural strokes with brush and ink that create visual forms with verbal meanings. A contemporary of such abstract expressionist gestural painters as Jackson Pollock, Ferber tried to give inert sculpture the same energy that one found in what came to be called "Action Painting." The

fluctuations in the copper surfaces catch light and intensify the sense of motion inherent in forms that seem to leap into space with something of the force of the Nike of Samothrace, now coming in for a landing at the top of a staircase in the Louvre. Placing the work, a gift from Edith Ferber, between the Williams museum staircases that lead up to Lawrence Hall from Spring Street makes this reference almost inescapable.

(East, Fayerweather, Prospect, Fitch, Currier, and Hopkins Observatory)

Yale University's South College provided the model for the original building of East College—a perfectly reasonable choice at a time when the water route to Yale (via the Connecticut River) was more convenient than the overland route to Harvard. (See full image, p. 17.)

31   East College
Tompson J. Skinner and Benjamin Skinner, builders, 1797–98

East College II
Architect unknown, 1842

The original East College was destroyed by fire in 1841. The fire started on a Sunday, while students were in church, across town in the Meeting House at Field Park. Fortunately, the appearance of the original East, opened in 1798, is preserved in old views of the campus, particularly a watercolor that shows the ramshackle appearance of the town, with unpaved Main Street headed east toward the Mohawk Trail, flanked by houses of varying sizes and designs and by the occasional fenced lot. (See detail of watercolor above.)

This structure was almost entirely given over to dormitory use, with the exception of some recitation spaces. The trustees decreed that the design should be based on the new South College at Yale, built in 1793. The plans and elevations of the two buildings are almost identical, with two entrances on each of the long sides that opened onto halls that separated living quarters. Students slept in small bedrooms off a larger shared living room heated by a fireplace. The four chimneys rising above the roof displayed the locations of the fireplaces. The four-story structure had ample natural light from the regular rows of rectangular windows punched into the thick brick walls that, together with the interior timber framing, held the building up. Longer than West, East was a large, plain, utilitarian structure paid for by a gift from the Massachusetts legislature of two townships in Maine, the sale of which provided the necessary funds.

The new East that replaced the one that burned was reduced in height to three stories out of fear for the safety of fourth-floor occupants, should another fire occur. The plan, with two doors in each of the long sides and suites with fireplaces for pairs of students, repeated that of the predecessor. In 1907 East was fancied up with the addition of robust Doric porches, made of white marble, to its original simple doorways. (See pp. 116–17.)

32   Fayerweather (South) Hall
Architect unknown, 1842; Addition: Allen & Collens, 1905

Fayerweather Hall, originally called South College, was erected in 1842 directly south of the new East College, to replace the space of the lost fourth story of the original East. Both East and South have flat roofs, a strange choice for a snowy climate that was probably dictated by a necessity for economy. For a brief moment in 1902, the college contemplated demolishing the homely building, as was suggested by the Olmsted brothers in their campus plan. But in 1905 the consulting architect Robert Peabody recognized the potential of South if incorporated into a formal quadrangle. (See entry 34, p. 134.) Williams, now serving a richer clientele, extended the south end of South with a suite of more spacious rooms, creating an enclave known as the Gold Coast. The

architects, Allen & Collens, coordinated the addition with their simultaneous construction of Fitch. At that time, the name of South was changed to Fayerweather to honor a donor. A remodeling of both dormitories in the 1950s inserted double-loaded corridors that rendered the elaborate Doric portals of 1905 useless, so they now lead, senselessly, to windows.

33   Hopkins Observatory
Professor Albert Hopkins with the assistance of students, 1835–38

Albert Hopkins, the younger brother of President Mark Hopkins, taught science at Williams. In the fall of 1834 he sailed for Liverpool on his own dime, entrusted by the college with $4,000 to acquire scientific apparatuses for teaching purposes. While there, he must have come in contact with the latest thinking in Europe about the design and construction of astronomical observatories. He went to Paris, but the equipment he brought back was all English. Returning to the college in the spring of 1835, he enlisted a group of students to help quarry local stone that they assembled into the building we now see: the oldest still-functioning observatory in the United States and one of the architectural gems of the campus.

Sited originally on the highest point of what is now the Berkshire Quadrangle, the building has a hexagonal central section to which two rectangular wings are attached. Although the bottom level appears on the outside to be a hexagon with two rectangular wings, the central space on the interior has cylindrical walls that support a hemispheric dome. This circle-in-a-hexagon, topped by a balustrade, is then extruded vertically into a wooden hexagon from which a slightly narrower wooden cylinder rises. The elegance of the proportions and the sympathy of the forms to each other indicate a love for mathematics and geometry on Albert Hopkins's part. It is a handsome building for an amateur architect and his student laborers. It is also sufficiently complex to give an architectural frisson to the attentive viewer. Did Hopkins actually conceive of this three-dimensional trick for reasons of architectural elegance and appropriateness? Or did things just turn out that way for functional reasons? Whatever he may have been thinking, Hopkins designed a building that telescopes.

The north side, parallel to Main Street and containing the original principal entrance, was treated more elegantly than the south. On the north the corners of the core are marked by carefully cut, gray granite quoins that stand out against the multicolored, rough stone quarried by Hopkins and his students. The elongated paired columns that frame the north door, which Hopkins must have copied from an architectural book, have the elegance of Robert Adam's work a few decades earlier. The south side was much less fancy: no quoins at the corners and no columns flanking what was clearly a back door. The modest

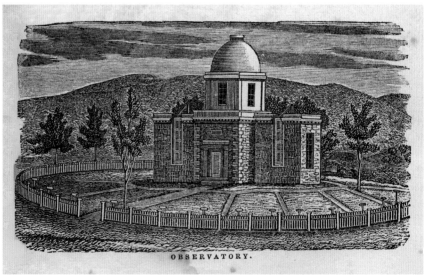

OBSERVATORY.

TOP **Hopkins Observatory, 1859** BOTTOM **Albert Hopkins drew on a long tradition of observatories set in centrally planned gardens, as shown in this woodcut of 1839.**

back side appears in a photo of 1859 that shows the building crawling with students in top hats.

The oldest view of the observatory, published on the cover of the course offerings for the 1839 academic year after it opened, shows it in its original condition. Instead of a cylinder at the top, there is a hemispheric dome that was destroyed in a windstorm in the winter of 1841. Surrounding the building's base are radial plantings that suggest a compass rose, a form that is repeated in correct form in the pavement of the central room at ground level. (A compass rose, if divided into at least sixteen sections, points to the four cardinal directions and to at least three other directions between two cardinal points: for instance, north-northeast, northeast, and east-northeast.) Among Albert Hopkins's many interests was horticulture, which he employed to give his observatory an appropriate setting. A decade later the college appointed him to design a garden in front of Lawrence Hall, the new library.

That setting of 1838 no longer exists; Hopkins Observatory has wandered. After Fitch was completed in 1908, the observatory was moved to the south end of the new quad and incorporated into Smedley Terrace, which finished off the rectangular design of the new Berkshire Quadrangle. When Prospect House was planned for that site, the observatory once again was picked up and moved in 1962, this time to the north end of the quad to overlook Main Street. At that time a somewhat cheesy replica of the columns flanking the north door was added to the south door, to turn the old back door into a new main entrance. The north door, partly hidden behind bushes and raised above ground level, is no longer usable as an entrance.

Hopkins sited the building parallel to Main Street, to maintain that line. Nature, however, did not cooperate, or—more properly—the original surveyors of Williamstown did not when they laid the town out on something close to, but not exactly, a true north–south line. The divergence is reflected in the observatory's structure. The roof of the east wing is cut on a diagonal by a narrow trough (now covered by a metal roof) that lies on the meridian as it passes over the quad. The tall windows in the north and south sides of the east wing do not line up with each other. That on the south is farther to the east than the one on the north. Inside the building, one can see that the two windows in the side walls and the trough in the roof are all connected. The north and south walls of the east wing, as well as the roof, could be opened up to observe the transit of stars across the meridian. Perhaps the cleverest part of the observatory design is the movability of the cylindrical drum that caps the building. The original crank that turns the drum is still in place and can be used to revolve it over the hexagonal base. Following the cylinder's motion, the telescope inside the drum turns on its own base to follow the movement of heavenly bodies.

Almost all the equipment that Hopkins purchased in England, including a grandfather clock or regulator, is still in the building, as are historic devices bought at later dates. A planetarium now occupies the circular room at the center of the ground floor. Celestial bodies today are projected electrically on a dome, which originally sported gold stars that depicted the constellations. There is no interior connection between the domed room on the ground floor and the wooden structures above; an outdoor stair has always been necessary to gain access to the upper level.

Hopkins was a deeply religious man. Over each entrance is a plaque, now almost illegible, that stresses the notion that the study of the heavens was a route to understand the glory of their creator. Hopkins paid the cost of $2,075 for the construction himself, and he built it without express permission from the trustees. A year after the building opened, however, they voted to reimburse him partially, since he insisted on contributing at least $500. At the same time they named the building the Hopkins Observatory.

34 Fitch Hall (Berkshire Hall)

Allen & Collens, 1905–6; Basement renovation: The Architects Collaborative, 1963

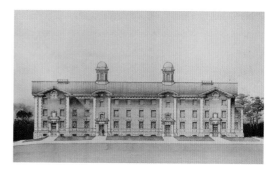

The Berkshire Quadrangle was conceived in 1902, when the Olmsted brothers urged that all future buildings of Williams College "be grouped in a series of quadrangles, with one side open toward Main Street," of which the "easternmost quadrangle would necessarily be on a knoll occupied by East and South Colleges" (the latter now Fayerweather). That same summer the alumni began to raise money for a new L-shaped dormitory that would define the quad. Alumni added a curious proviso: the student rooming fees earned by the dorm should be used to supplement the faculty's "absurdly low compensation."

Berkshire Hall (later Fitch) was the subject of Williams College's only full-fledged architectural competition. Benjamin Wistar Morris, a Paris-trained architect who had worked on the designs of the New York Public Library, seems to have been amused by the challenge of marking each entry with as many architectural motifs as possible.

In recognition of the signal importance of the new dormitory, the college authorized, for the first and only time in its history, an architectural competition. In the spring of 1905, seven entries arrived, some by the leading architects of the day, including Delano & Aldrich, Cady & Berg, and Benjamin Wistar Morris. Several of these firms exhibited their entries at the Architectural League in New York and even published them in professional journals.

But their ornate neo-Georgian proposals were rejected in favor of a much more prosaic design by Francis Allen, also a competitor but one who had the advantage of having already built half a dozen buildings for the college. Before construction began, a fateful change was made. Robert Peabody (of Peabody & Stearns), who was serving as the trustees' architectural adviser, recommended that the new dormitory run parallel to South College, which would then be extended to serve as the pendant to Berkshire. At their meeting in June 1905 the trustees agreed. Allen modified his L-shaped building accordingly, making it a plain brick rectangle. At the same time, as Peabody had recommended, he enlarged South College with an addition so scrupulously matched that one must search to find the seam. Finally, he outfitted both buildings with stately marble porticos, giving the Berkshire Quadrangle its splendid unifying theme: simple brick buildings with festive marble porticos, not touching at the corners but open to admit diagonal views toward the surrounding mountains.

In 1963 The Architects Collaborative received its first commission from the college, the renovation of the basement of Berkshire into social spaces required by the Sawyer administration to convert the existing dormitory into an enhanced residential group. Students in that new unit elected to change its name to Fitch, in honor of the college's first president, to whom no building had been dedicated. They wanted to be able to call themselves "Sons of Fitch."

Currier Hall

35   Currier Hall

Robins & Oakman, 1908–9

Currier Hall, the fourth and final dormitory of the Berkshire Quadrangle, is the most important Williams College building designed by an alumnus. John S. Oakman was one of two architects produced by the Class of 1899 (the other was Edward Crosby Doughty), and he studied architecture at the École des Beaux-Arts in Paris and later in the office of Carrère & Hastings, New York City. There he learned an elegant and refined classicism of which Currier's exterior gives no hint. His goal was to complete the quad as a unified ensemble, and he designed what was effectively a twin of East. Only to the east, where the site drops sharply and the building requires a mighty stone base, does Currier depart dramatically from its model.

The completion of the quad in 1909 was a milestone for Williams College, and its Colonial Revival architecture provided a model for the next half century. But it was also a model for a new kind of gentlemanly college life, in which the nineteenth-century gulf between professor and student would be bridged. The new president, Harry A. Garfield, announced that he would eat his meals at Currier Hall, which would form "a new center of college life, to be joined in by both Faculty and students."[3] He announced the new policy at an alumni dinner attended by his friend Woodrow Wilson, who clearly endorsed Garfield's declaration that "colleges must not be mere country clubs in which to breed up a leisure class."[4]

Currier Hall's grand ballroom was once its dining hall.

In fact, Currier was very much like a country club. Its common room and adjoining 110-seat dining room were "finely finished in paneled Cathedral oak"; over the door between them hung a portrait of President Henry Hopkins, while other portraits adorned its walls. Cathedral oak is not cheap. Currier cost $118,000 to house thirty-two students, while Fitch cost $106,000 to house forty-two, leaving enough left over to enlarge South Hall (Fayerweather). Today, the Currier Ballroom, as it is now known, remains one of the most luxurious spaces on the Williams campus. It is one of the paradoxes of Currier that this jewel box of a space—where Oakman applied the sophisticated details he learned while working on the New York Public Library with Carrère & Hastings—is essentially unknown to the public.

Although Oakman keenly pursued work at Williams, he was never given a second chance, other than some desperately needed repairs at Jesup. But even buried in a footnote, his epitaph is a proud one: the architect-alumnus who led Williams out of the Victorian era.

36 Prospect House
Shepley Bulfinch Richardson and Abbot, 1960–62

Prospect House, President Baxter's first foray into architectural modernism (still under construction when Sawyer took over), was a timid step. A four-story wall of a building on its northern, or quad, side, Prospect is characterized by a triple repetition of a triadic motif of wide entrance bays flanked by narrow window bays. Any Beaux-Arts-trained architect (note the basic similarity to nearby Fitch) could have come up with that arrangement, but might have enlivened it by varying the central bay. In this midcentury modern design by Jean Paul Carlihan of the Shepley Bulfinch Richardson and Abbot firm, unbroken brick verticals alternate with recessed window or door bays of white wood and casement windows. A low shed roof, surmounted by three chimneys, tops off this ever so modest and mannerly design. On the south side Prospect responds to a slope by reaching down to a fifth floor at ground level.

37   Driscoll Dining Hall

Shepley Bulfinch Richardson and Abbot, 1963

Driscoll Dining Hall—its construction approved by the trustees in January 1963—marks the initial step the college took to create a new eating space to serve two new residential houses that would replace the fraternities. Prospect Hall, already in use, was one house, and Berkshire (now Fitch), with a renovated basement housing social spaces, was the second.

    Sawyer was in a hurry to establish a functioning example of his intentions for the whole campus; the building, which opened just after Thanksgiving, went from authorization to occupation in less than a year. Driscoll was, thanks to Sawyer's influence, the first really modern building on campus and really the only one to owe a considerable debt to Frank Lloyd Wright. Although the commission went to the same conservative Boston firm that designed Prospect—and landed on the drawing board of Jean Paul Carlihan, the man who had created that modest building—the switch in presidents from Baxter to Sawyer allowed Carlihan to give free rein to his modernist tendencies. He based his stacked and interlocked cylinders on such unbuilt Wright projects of the 1950s as the Jester House.

The exterior is clad in rough-cut blocks of the same limestone used in the basement of Currier, to create a sort of a primitive fortress at what was then the edge of campus. At the upper, or entrance, level a circular hall gives access to a curving staircase that descends to the serving line and dining rooms below. Two doors to either side of the staircase void open into the ends of a crescent-shaped living room surrounded by floor-to-ceiling windows that look southeast into treetops. On the lower level, twin circular dining rooms, with radially laid beams in their ceilings, also offer views into the woods. The living room, centered on a cylindrical fireplace, is a bit disconcerting, because from one end it is impossible to look around the fireplace to see what is happening in the other. But the dining rooms provide a pleasant atmosphere for eating in the serene but cozy enclosure of the circles.

38 Spencer Studio Art Building
Carlos Jimenez with Cambridge Seven Associates, 1996

For the decades after the 1950s, when the teaching of studio art became a serious part of the Williams curriculum, the program was an architectural orphan with no permanent home. Studios had been located in the basement of the 1920s addition to Lawrence, in parts of Goodrich, in a garage off Spring Street, in the underpinnings of the Greylock dining hall, in a corner of the Chandler Gymnasium later assigned to the basketball coach, or wherever else a spare room might be found. When the Moore addition was attached to Lawrence, a well-lit space on the lowest level was designated for studios, but within a year or two reassigned to museum storage. The situation seemed hopeless, until Jack Wadsworth (Class of 1961) came along to donate a new facility for studio teaching only.

In the search in 1991 for an architect capable of designing a building with the requisite aesthetic finesse, eight architects or firms were interviewed, including the relatively unknown Carlos Jimenez from Houston. How he came to the committee's attention is a lesson in how important it is for young architects to get their work published. In a New York bookstore a member of the selection committee ran across a small volume, just published, on Jimenez's work, with an admiring introduction by the guru of European Postmodernism, the Italian architect Aldo Rossi. The book persuaded a group of artists and art historians from the Williams Art Department to go to Houston to look at his work. When they walked into a small studio building by Jimenez, one artist exclaimed, "I want to work here!" Jimenez got the job.

Since Jimenez, a native of Costa Rica and a resident of Texas, had never worked in a cold climate, he was paired with Cambridge Seven Associates to take on the challenges of New England winters. The result is a building with an irregular, U-shaped plan, with the broadest facade facing the

Spencer Studio's stair hall, a favorite site for student installations

source of north light, a sine qua non of studio space, and the arms embracing a courtyard to the south. Buff-colored stone cladding differentiates Spencer from other buildings on campus. The entrance at the northwest corner leads into a three-story hall that announces the theme of light that plays out in endless variations in the entire structure. Sculpture is housed in the two-story southeast corner, with a huge door that can be raised to allow students to haul their work outside to the courtyard to see it in daylight. Printmaking, with its heavy equipment, is on the ground floor to the north, lit by a long row of strip windows. Above that are the painting studios, with their huge panels of glass separated by the darker stone pilasters that appear to support a metal overhang. The purpose of this inclined plane is not clear, since there is little need to shade the north-facing windows below from the sun, but it is an essential visual element. The giant cantilever at the northwest corner announces the entrance with singular clarity, while the strip window above it signals the presence of faculty offices. The gently curved roof, a typical Jimenez detail, covers the three-story west wing, with classrooms for photography, video, architecture, and drawing, as well as faculty offices. Long corridors provide walls for students to hang up their work, and there is a small gallery at ground level for constantly changing public exhibitions. When school is in session, the building enjoys close to twenty-four-hour use.

39 Heating Plant

R. D. Kimball, 1903–4; Densmore, Le Clear & Robbins, 1931–32; Lockwood Greene Co., 1953

For its first century, Williams College heated all its buildings, including dormitories, by fireplaces or stoves in the individual rooms. There was no central heating plant until 1903. In that year the college commissioned R. D. Kimball, a Boston engineer, to design a heating plant large enough for four 125-horsepower boilers, enough to pipe steam heat to every campus building, including the houses of the professors. He also designed the round brick chimney, 125 feet high. The building still stands, a sturdy work of utilitarian architecture, if somewhat bewildered by its gigantic replacement.

Although Kimball's original plant was enlarged within a few years, it did not keep pace with the growing college. In 1931 a new heating plant was needed, and the commission was given to Densmore, Le Clear & Robbins, the architects who had recently enlarged Lasell Gymnasium. Their design translated the Georgian Revival of Ralph Adams Cram's earlier work, such as Chapin and Stetson, into industrial terms; the result was a severe cubic mass, softened somewhat by a classical cornice and a limestone belt course. These details irked Karl Weston, the head of the Williams Art Department, who felt that it was inappropriate to build a heating plant, a building type unknown to the ancient world, in a classical style. "In any building," he argued, "the architecture should express its function, and grow out of its purpose."

ABOVE **Williams College's 1931 heating plant was the occasion of its first architectural controversy. Should a decidedly modern building type be decked out in the trappings of colonial architecture? While the president and the architects fussed over the classical cornice, it was the soaring pair of smokestacks that gave the building its expressive power.**

Many students and professors found Weston's argument sympathetic. It was the college's first serious debate about the place of modern architecture on its historic campus, and the controversy embarrassed the administration, especially when it reached the pages of the *Boston Globe*. Cram was nominally the college's consulting architect, but it seems that no one had bothered to show him Densmore's designs for the new building. Now he was hastily brought in to pass belated judgment. To the relief of President Garfield, the modernist-leaning Cram declared that the power plant, with its mighty industrially scaled windows, "does express its function outwardly." But he chided the college as well: had he seen the drawings earlier, he would have recommended the elimination of the classical cornice.

Densmore's design was built without changes, but it too was soon outstripped by growing demand. In 1953 a third bay was added to house a third boiler. The engineers of the Lockwood Greene Co. carefully matched Densmore's original building, although they simplified the windows and added what they termed "less filigree." The third bay can be easily spotted. All in all, it is a beautifully realized piece of industrial architecture that does precisely what it should do: speak poetically of the bold and purposeful harnessing of energy. If Lockwood Greene enlarged Densmore's building sympathetically, the same cannot be said about the subsequent engineers who have added to the building in recent years.

40 Faculty Artist Studios
Burr and McCallum, 1985

Artists on the Williams faculty have had as dicey a time finding places to do

their own work as finding
suitable spaces to teach
their students. One attempt
to ameliorate this situation
was the building of a small
structure to provide studios
for two artists, squeezed
onto a tiny, remote part of
campus near the heating
plant. Commissioned to
design the building were
Andy Burr (Class of 1966)
and his wife and partner,
Ann McCallum, both of
whom were teaching
undergraduate architecture
studio courses at the time.
Burr and McCallum dote on
the industrial vernacular
of New England, echoes of
which are clear in the elegant
simplicity of this building.
The gabled roof that covers

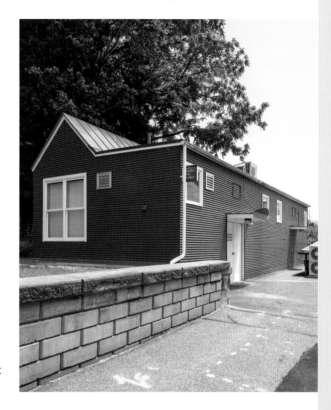

half of it provides a raised plane for the north-facing skylights that flood the
studios below with daylight. The oversized square windows, set directly into
the corrugated metal siding, not only provide light but also give the studios a
commanding sense of scale, despite their modest proportions.

ENDNOTES

1   *Williams Quarterly*, June 1857, 386.

2   Calvin Durfee, *A History of Williams College* (Boston: A. Williams, 1860), 302–3.

3   *Report of Harry Augustus Garfield, President of Williams College, for the Academic Year 1908–1909* (Williamstown, MA: Williams College, 1909), 11.

4   "New Ideas for College Life," *Morning News, Wilmington, Delaware*, February 19, 1909, 7.

Northeast Quadrant

41　Hopkins Hall

Francis R. Allen (Kenway & Allen), 1889–90; Alterations and additions: Architectural Resources Cambridge, 1988

It is amusing that the college's main administration building looks like no other building on campus. (See p. 8.) Hopkins Hall is an inspired performance in the style of Henry Hobson Richardson, America's champion of the modern Romanesque, and it has all his characteristic features: rock-faced masonry, heroically oversized round arches, passages of dense floral ornament. The style had a brief vogue in the 1880s, but by the time Hopkins was begun, it was already waning. Had Hopkins been built even a few years later, it would have looked quite different.

When President Mark Hopkins died in 1887, grieving alumni vowed to raise a memorial fund of $100,000. The goal was ambitious, but within a year the money was there—enough to build a new hall for "lectures, recitations, executive and other business."[1] The final $25,000 was contributed by Frederick Ferris Thompson, whose family had founded the Chase National Bank and who had attended Williams from 1852 to 1854 ("the best years of my life"). Thompson was promptly made head of the building committee, giving him the right to name the architect. He chose, not unreasonably, Francis Allen, the man who designed his summer house at Canandaigua, New York. So began a happy relationship that would ultimately give Williams eight Allen-designed buildings, most of them paid for by Thompson and his family.

With a generous welcoming arch on the side and a discouragingly narrow and steep entrance in the front, Hopkins Hall seems not to know which way to face. In fact, the entrances were carefully arranged to take into account the two functions of the original building. The front of the first floor was reserved for the college administration, with the treasurer's office to the right and the president at the base of the corner tower—in the projection that wisecracking students dubbed "the presidential bulge." Official visitors could enter from the front without ever crossing the paths of

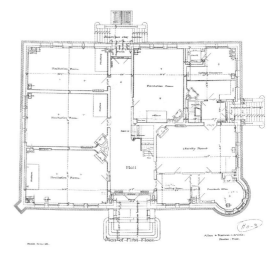

Hopkins Hall, first-floor plan of the original building

the students who clamored through the larger east and west entrances, making their way to the classrooms at the rear and the upper stories.

The best feature of Hopkins is its luxuriant palette of materials: a base of pink granite, a first story of rugged local dolomite, walls of buff Pompeiian brick, and trim in red Longmeadow sandstone from quarries near Springfield. But what one generation found a stirring Romanesque citadel, the next found a dowdy Victorian set piece. There were repeated proposals to move it back from Main Street to make room for a building of more reputable character. In 1936 Ralph Adams Cram proposed a Colonial Revival facelift that would have brought it into harmony with Chapin and Stetson, but the college bridled at paying for merely cosmetic work, especially during the Great Depression. The building survived unchanged until 1988, when the town building inspector, alarmed at its dilapidated condition, ordered it closed. President Francis Oakley, who had vowed to be a nonbuilding president, was compelled to give Hopkins a thoroughgoing renovation. Architectural Resources Cambridge extracted and replaced the entire historic interior, its wood-paneled classrooms, with a sleekly mirrored contemporary interior. To the north they built an extension that reinterpreted Hopkins in Postmodern terms, the details flattened and made graphic, as if cut by stencils. Faculty wags, noting the mirror surfaces and air-conditioned interiors, immediately redubbed the building Hopkins Mall.

Cram would have given Hopkins Hall a new crown, but Architectural Resources Cambridge did the opposite and performed an architectural root canal. In either case, it has now become impossible to imagine Williams College without Hopkins, and one would no more banish it from the campus than one would banish an ancient but beloved family dog.

42 Thompson Memorial Chapel
Allen & Collens, 1903–5

Williams has one building of an exceptional interest…the Thompson Memorial Chapel, an interesting and scholarly and picturesque design in the "decorated" phase of English Gothic.
—Montgomery Schuyler (*Architectural Record*, 1910)

I have moments of wanting to have the tower lie down and the church stand up.
—Whitney Stoddard

When Montgomery Schuyler, the acerbic dean of American architecture criticism, visited Williams College, only one building emerged unscathed: Thompson Memorial Chapel. It stood out when he wrote in 1910 and still stands out today. It is the only campus building to be explicitly modeled on a historical prototype, the fifteenth-century church of St. Cuthbert's, in Wells, England. It is the only building deemed so important that another building—Griffin Hall—was moved to make room for it. And it is the only one with a substantial program of architectural sculpture and stained glass.

The donor was Mary Clark Thompson, whose husband, Frederick Ferris Thompson, gave Williams the trio of buildings known as the Thompson Laboratories. They had no children, and when Frederick Thompson died in 1899, his widow received the bulk of his estate. He had drawn up a second will in case he outlived his wife, and this one provided for numerous charitable bequests. And although she was under no legal obligation to do so, Mary Clark Thompson—to the surprise of nearly everyone—decided to fund those bequests anyway.

One of them was for a new chapel for Williams College to replace the cramped and dated chapel of 1859. The commission was given to Francis Allen, the architect who handled all the Thompson family buildings. He was practicing with a much younger partner, Charles Collens, thirty years his junior, who brought an entirely new sensibility to the firm. One need only stand between Hopkins Hall and Thompson Chapel to see the difference. Collens was a product of the École des Beaux-Arts in Paris and brought academic discipline and restraint to the firm. He took his cue from the new dormitories at Princeton

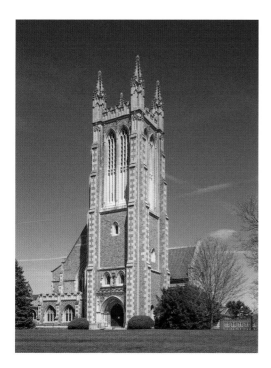

University and Bryn Mawr College that established the fashion for the Collegiate Gothic style, marked by polygonal bays, leaded-glass windows, and crenelated turrets, all drawn together in gently rambling compositions. Collens even shipped from Philadelphia the same glistening mica-rich stone used at Princeton and Bryn Mawr, known locally as Wissahickon schist. The result was a tasteful, scholarly medievalism, a style at which Collens was quite adept and that would recur in his most famous work, the Cloisters in New York (1931–38).

Construction began in 1903, and two years later the chapel was complete. As picturesque as the composition is, the spatial sequence is a thing of exquisite refinement: the visitor enters at the base of the prominent tower, turns left to enter a generously scaled narthex—and then turns right to pass through the entrance arch. After the low space of the narthex follows the broad and lofty nave, whose central aisle leads to the polygonal chancel at the far end, with its elaborately ribbed vault. But before reaching the chancel, the nave first expands into a spacious crossing, with a pair of short but wide transepts. The whole space is of exceptional richness, with gorgeous carved pews, slender limestone columns, and a magnificent hammer-beam truss, each beam of which comes to rest above a graceful carved angel.

With its stress on ceremonial movement toward a place of sacred solemnity, Thompson Memorial Chapel is emphatically a processional building. Its use of space could not differ more from Goodrich Chapel, which was a space of communal gathering. But that chapel was built in 1859 when Williams

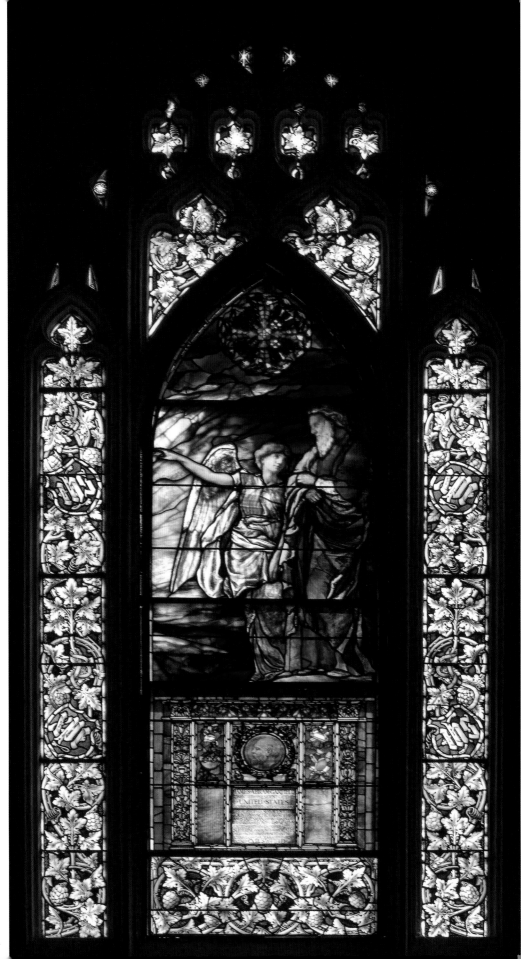

was still a sectarian college and was emphatically Congregationalist. By the turn of the century this was no longer true. According to a census of 1911, the 72 Congregationalist students attending Williams were outnumbered both by Episcopalians (116) and by Presbyterians (78). Under the circumstances, it was inevitable that the chapel strike a different architectural note than its predecessor. If Goodrich was a theological statement, carefully upholding Congregationalist orthodoxy, Thompson Chapel was a social statement, inviting students to worship together in an ecumenical culture of genteel Protestantism. Its hallmarks are comfort, prosperity, and ease.

But because the college was still officially Congregationalist, with compulsory chapel attendance for students, the artistic embellishment of the chapel was explicitly Christian, and centered on the life and teachings of Christ. This was expressed in the rich stained-glass program, chosen in consultation with Mary Clark Thompson and executed by the Church Glass and Decorating Company, of New York. It is of extraordinarily high aesthetic quality. The great window to the south illustrates the seven corporal works of mercy (e.g., feed the hungry, visit the sick, redeem the captive, shelter the homeless). The west transept depicts Christ's injunction to spread the gospel and shows his apostles embarking on their mission, such as Philip departing for Phrygia, Peter for Antioch, Paul for Greece, Thomas for Carthage, and James the Less for Jerusalem. The east transept addresses the modern world by depicting the forces of nature. There Christ is depicted as Creator of the Universe, as he commands the angels to carry the four great forces—light, heat, motion, and electricity—to man. Below is an image of Adam. The choir shows angels bearing musical instruments, while the windows of the aisles, appropriately close to where the students sat, are inspiring images of professions (and not always the most lucrative): law, poetry, music, and navigation, among others.

The single most important work of art in the chapel is the memorial window to American president James A. Garfield, located in the southwest corner of the west transept. The work of John LaFarge, it is made almost entirely of "opalescent glass," LaFarge's invention for producing exquisitely layered and vibrant color. It was commissioned immediately after the assassination of the president in 1881 and was completed the following year; originally installed in Goodrich Hall, it was moved to Thompson upon its completion. Above a medallion with a portrait of Garfield is an image of an angel showing Moses a vision of the Promised Land—an appropriate symbol for the martyred president who, like Moses, did not live to complete his journey. At the apex of the window is an intriguing feature, "a wheel formed of many-colored glasses with cruciform spokes, adapted from the 'Wheel of Law' of Eastern religions," placed there, LaFarge claimed, for decorative purposes, but also showing his growing interest in world religion. The window was the gift of Cyrus W. Field, the creator of the transatlantic telegraph cable.

John LaFarge, Garfield memorial window, 1882

As a memorial chapel, the building contains several notable ones, including a marker to Ephraim Williams, whose remains were transferred there in 1920. In the chancel is the roster of names of Williams students and alumni who died in America's wars (and one who died in the Spanish Civil War).

There is one curious addendum to the story. The same bequest that provided Thompson Chapel also provided for a new library building at Vassar, which was designed at the same time, by the same architects, and much in the same style. Evidently, the overworked architects kept their reference books open to St. Cuthbert's—an odd architectural case of fraternal twins, separated at birth.

43 Griffin Hall (New Chapel)
Edward Dorr Griffin (?), 1827–28; Removal and remodeling: Harding & Seaver, 1904; Interior remodeling: Childs Bertman Tseckares, 1997

Confirming the bravura statement of President Edward Dorr Griffin and the trustees that Williams College would endure despite the calamity of 1821, when President Zephaniah Swift Moore resigned and half the student body decamped for other institutions, Griffin Hall rises proudly on the eastern eminence to stun the visitor approaching from the east with its scale and architectural sophistication. Unlike the two earlier buildings at the college, the new chapel turned its facade parallel to Main Street to catch the sun and form a wall between the town and the mountains to the north. Its gilded dome, raised above a two-story, octagonal cupola, brought a degree of architectural elegance and drama to a town that had hardly known such things.

At a special meeting on November 19, 1822, in Griffin's second year as president, the trustees voted unanimously to "erect a College chapel," doubtless at Griffin's behest. In doing so, they resurrected a plan to build a new chapel that first surfaced in September 1811 and was on the verge of being realized in 1814, just before the uncertainties created by a possible relocation

of the college to Hampshire County put an end to the project. Griffin would have known about this proposal by reading the trustees' minutes, to which he surely had access. Raising the money continued to be difficult, because of the nagging question of the college's ultimate location. Once the state legislature

decided in 1825 that a move was illegal, Griffin swiftly raised $25,000 within a year to build a chapel and endow a professorship. He attributed the seemingly miraculous fundraising to divine intervention. "God himself has reared it. It has been erected by the Holy Ghost," Griffin proclaimed in the sermon that he preached at its dedication on October 2, 1828. The choice of site had come late in the game. The first thought had been to locate the new chapel on the opposite side of the street, either east or west of East College, as had been proposed in 1811. The final decision to use the present site was made by the trustees in the summer of 1827. The building must have gone up rapidly to be ready for a dedication only a year and a few months later.

The facade of Griffin Hall is divided into three sections by a projecting central element topped by a classical pediment—the first appearance of that ancient form on a campus that came to enjoy many another. Emphasis on the center continues in the large, elegant fanlight inside the pediment. Fanlights illuminate interiors of buildings, but here the light enters into an unused attic. It is pure showmanship. The commanding cupola, dome, and weather vane complete the splashy vertical axis. Apparently, Griffin himself stood across Main Street and directed workmen in the precise placement of the crosspieces of the weather vane.

The tripartite division of the facade has only to do with making the view from the street impressive. It reveals nothing of the arrangement of interior

Edward Dorr Griffin (?), Phelps House, Andover, Massachusetts, ca. 1820. The house that Griffin built while teaching at Andover Theological Seminary features a round-arched arcade on the ground floor. Arches supported by square piers are characteristic of masonry architecture. To reproduce them in wood, as they are here, perhaps betrays an amateur's misunderstanding of an architectural form, the same kind of architectural "mistake" that one finds in the fanlight that uselessly illuminates the attic of Griffin Hall.

spaces. To the left of the center rose the two-story chapel itself, the raison d'être of the structure, whose presence is clearly suggested only on the west side, where a simplified Palladian window provides a clue to what goes on behind the otherwise regular arrangement of rectangular windows punched in a brick wall. As old photographs show, the facade originally boasted two simple doors that gave no sense of what lay behind them. From Trustees' Meeting minutes one learns that on the ground floor there was a laboratory to the southeast, adjacent to a northeast room, and in the chapel a central aisle flanked by pews. President Hopkins provided much more information about the interior disposition in his 1859 sermon at the dedication of a second new chapel, now Goodrich Hall, across the street. Hopkins, who began work at the college in the fall of 1825, had known the building from the start of its construction. He stated that in addition to the chapel, it also contained a library, cabinet for philosophical apparatuses, conference room, senior recitation room, room for the libraries of the (student) societies, chemical laboratory, and lecture room. Small wonder that it was three stories tall.

The reticence of the building to proclaim its primary function is curious. Griffin wanted to separate the college's religious space from its dormitory spaces, a problem in all-purpose West College, where mischievous students in residence could easily wreak havoc on the holy. He economized by including many necessary spaces in the same building as the chapel. In his dedicatory sermon, Griffin made clear his priorities: "It would be sacrilege to apply the building to the uses of mere unhallowed science, or to any other interest than that of God. Let it be devoted to science as subservient to the Redeemer's kingdom." The original two doors in the south facade, heretofore inexplicable, acknowledged the dual dedication of the building to the spiritual and the scientific that Griffin stressed in his dedicatory sermon. The western door led to the chapel, the more frequently used eastern door to the diverse rooms where the teaching of science and many other activities took place. The growth of the science curriculum led in 1845 to an awkward one-story addition to the east of a room for instruction in chemistry.

Griffin wasted no money on the rear of the building, which could not be seen from the street. Whereas he used handsome granite lintels over the east, south, and west windows, on the north side there are flat brick arches like the ones on West and East. The building's south front rises out of the ground on carefully carved limestone courses, but the foundation at the rear was made of rough, irregular blocks, hacked from the jagged stone outcroppings that had to be cleared to prepare the site.

The chapel had galleries, and probably a pulpit raised up to a level just below the bottom of the simplified Palladian window that surrounded the preacher with light that could be taken as divine. As Whitney Stoddard suggested, the interior was likely based on a "Design for a Meeting House" by the Greenfield architect Asher Benjamin, in his book *The Country Builder's Assistant* (1805), which Griffin could easily have known. Another source of inspiration was Bulfinch Hall (1818) at Phillips Academy, Andover, although Griffin did not capture the elegant refinement of the prototype, with its round arched windows and delicate keystones on the second floor. While teaching at Andover Theological Seminary, Griffin probably designed and certainly had built a large, quite elegant house for himself, financed by a rich donor; it is now the residence of the headmaster of Andover. That experience must have given him the courage to take on the challenge of designing a much larger structure.

The multipurpose interior has been refigured several times. The first major intervention occurred after 1859, when the college opened a new, entirely freestanding stone chapel across the street, now known as Goodrich Hall. The original chapel, pace Griffin, became a display area for a natural history

TOP **Griffin Hall's faculty room originally served as the college chapel.**
BOTTOM **Watercolor of design for new entrance to Griffin Hall, Harding & Seaver, 1904**

collection. Then, in 1904, the entire structure was moved forty feet to the northeast to make room for the present Thompson Memorial Chapel that rose to its west. At that point Harding & Seaver, the Pittsfield architects, replaced the two entrance doors of Griffin with the present single, classical confection, shown in their exacting watercolor, that is based on the original north door of the Hopkins Observatory.

That door has received its share of modernist criticism as inappropriate to the period of the original building. Stoddard recalled driving Frank Lloyd Wright in 1933 into Williamstown to give a lecture. As they passed Griffin, Wright asked, "Who put that damned door on that quite nice building?" Or rather, that is the decorous way Whitney quoted Wright in print. In conversation, Whitney put less genteel words in Wright's mouth: "Who fucked up that quite nice building with that damned door?" Wright, of course, would not have known that the doorway of Griffin's house in Andover looks a lot like what Harding & Seaver applied to Griffin almost a hundred years later. At Andover he had a wealthy merchant from Marblehead willing to foot his architectural bills. At Williamstown he had no such fat-cat support.

The present central staircase seems to go with the new central portal. Also in 1904 Harding & Seaver refigured the chapel interior into something like what one finds there now. The natural history objects were removed, and their display cases, apparently inserted under the galleries at the time of the conversion to a natural history space, were updated to hold law books. The room became both a classroom and the site of faculty meetings. The most recent reconfiguration by CBT, particularly clumsy, removed the bookcases to make the space at ground level more capacious to house the meetings of a growing faculty. The elegance of the space is seriously compromised by the current imitation gas-light fixtures that look as if they were picked off a shelf at Home Depot or Lowe's. The same firm completely refitted the classroom interiors, swapping the ancient desks carved with the initials of generations of students for new furnishings to go with the up-to-date electronic equipment a contemporary classroom requires. Couldn't those desks, with the sense of history they contained, have coexisted with new technology to create a far richer classroom experience?

44 Soldier's Monument
James G. Batterson, sculptor, 1866–68; Cram & Ferguson, architects, 1928

By 1863 it was already clear that the Civil War would claim a good many Williams College alumni, and a committee was formed to build a monument to record their names. A prominent site was found to the east of Griffin. The Boston architect Joseph R. Richards designed the octagonal base, twenty feet high, in a suitably solemn Gothic style, with buttresses at each corner and steep gables. James G. Batterson, a Hartford builder with a lucrative sideline in Civil War memorials, provided the bronze soldier above. (It was Batterson's standard sentry, versions of which can be found across New England.) The monument was dedicated in 1868, bearing the name of twenty-nine Civil War dead.

It stood in that form for only sixty years. It might have survived longer (colleges tamper reluctantly with their landmarks), except that a new memorial to the college's war dead was built in Thompson Chapel after World War I. After the names of the Civil War dead were recorded there, the brownstone base of the Soldier's Monument became redundant. That base also happened to be

the most dated part, an item of mid-Victorian funereal art more appropriate to a cemetery. In 1927 President Harry Garfield decided to spare the statue but destroy its base. He entrusted the task to Alexander Hoyle, whom he knew and respected as Cram & Ferguson's partner in charge of designing Stetson Library. In place of the gloomy Gothic base, Hoyle devised an elegantly tapered granite pedestal. Note how it subtly shifts from solid and classical moldings at the base to abstract Art Deco reeding at the top: a graceful Jazz Age plinth for Batterson's mournful bronze sentinel.

45   Schapiro and Hollander Halls
Bohlin Cywinski Jackson, 2007–8

Schapiro and Hollander Halls form a fascinating case study in planning. Peter Bohlin had to build replacements for both an outdated library and faculty offices, using more or less the same sites, but there was a catch: there could be no interruption of service. His first step was to build new offices to receive the professors hunkering in the former stacks of Stetson Library. Until this happened, Bohlin could not demolish the old stacks to build a new library in their place. The scheme envisioned something analogous to castling in chess: the dislodged offices would move to the west while the library shifted to the east. At that point, Sawyer could vanish and Schapiro and Hollander Halls could stand free, a new academic quadrangle emerging between them, the eastern termination of a new monumental axis that now extended all the way to the

Schapiro Hall, east facade

'62 Center for Theatre and Dance in the west. Their role was to define that quadrangle and to serve as the eastern gateway to the axis.

Bohlin decidedly did not want traditional office buildings with prim corridors and a formal division between public and private spaces. Instead he designed loosely flowing public passages that sometimes widen into a space of gathering or narrow into a hall, seamlessly and without transition; hallways terminate in glazed walls. Having recently designed a series of all-glass Apple stores, he used a great deal of glass in the new buildings, opening up views into nature in every direction. (And in exchange, nature itself was invited onto the buildings in the form of green roofs.)

The most conspicuous feature of the two academic buildings is the profusion of materials—metal, wood, glass, even Vermont slate. During one memorable meeting with the building committee, the architects were asked if the different faces of their buildings could be given more unity by means of continuous belt courses and cornices so that the two buildings would look more like a single discrete object. "We don't make objects" was the answer, only semijocular. This explains the various approaches to the different facades, each generated by its particular circumstances. The east facade of Schapiro Hall enjoys an attractive view and was given a continuous plane of glass. The quadrangle suggested a more formal rhythm and was carried out in brick, although the south-facing windows were given projecting hoods to screen them from the sun. The two blocks facing the classical library are the most formal of all, abstract porticos of brick piers standing at attention and serving as a ceremonial frame to the axis. But on the west side of Hollander, as if to compensate for this excessive exercise in logic, all hell breaks loose. Here is the so-called helmet room, a metal-clad pod projecting from the building. President Morty Schapiro was not fond of the feature, and for a time there was a vain attempt to mask it with landscaping. A decade later, no one gives it a second glance.

46 Sawyer Library (Stetson Library and Chapin Library)
Cram & Ferguson, 1919–22; Addition: Cram & Ferguson, 1955–56; Bohlin Cywinski Jackson Architects, 2011–14

The original Stetson Library began as part of President Garfield's effort to reshape the college into a progressive modern institution. Crucial to this was a modern library, as he announced in his annual report of 1911:

> The present library facilities are extremely inadequate. Lawrence Hall is overcrowded and books are distributed over the campus in two branch libraries and in the several laboratories. The buildings are not fireproof and the arrangement is wasteful in the matter of service and of time necessarily occupied in using books so widely distributed. A new central library building is needed, commodiously arranged, with ample allowance for increase in the number of volumes, and as secure against fire as possible.

Already President Garfield had privately asked Ralph Adams Cram, then designing Chapin Hall, to think ahead about where a new library might go. Cram proposed a site at the eastern edge of the campus where the ground falls steeply toward Southworth Street, which would permit the placement of several "recitation rooms" on the downhill side beneath the library proper. Working with this site, he prepared a preliminary design in 1915. Then came the crisis. Cram had planned his library to have "an alcove or subdivision" to display the rare-book collection of Alfred C. Chapin. But when Chapin visited Harvard's newly built Widener Library, which had just such a memorial alcove to the donor's son, who drowned on the *Titanic*, he was appalled at the "gangs of ignorant curious people" who came to gawk. Chapin wanted to spare his collection such a fate. In late 1915 he broke the bad news to Bentley Warren, the trustee who headed the building committee. Instead of a room in the new library, Chapin now demanded "a separate structure—not, perhaps, much larger—if at all—than the AΔΦ [i.e., Perry House] acceptable architecturally—fire-proof—burglar proof."

This shocked Garfield and Warren, who scrambled to keep Chapin from doing something impulsive. They reminded him that Cram's plans were provisional and that another architect still might be chosen. And until the plan of the library was settled, they could hardly authorize Chapin's separate building. Warren clearly did not want a private museum that looked confusingly like a fraternity house. Why not a sublime Roman temple, like the Maison Carrée in

Nîmes? Or perhaps a pair of Maisons Carrées, one to each side of the library? So the alarmed Warren wrote to a friend, asking if he happened to remember the dimensions of the Maison Carrée.

Garfield, equally alarmed, asked his brother Abram for advice. Abe, as he was known, graduated from Williams College in 1893 and had an architectural practice in Cleveland; he also knew classical architecture. He informed his brother that the temple of Fortuna Virilis in Rome was a better model than the Maison Carrée (if only because four Ionic columns are cheaper than six Corinthian columns). But even at $48,000, the temple building would have diverted needed resources away from Cram's large library. A frustrated President Garfield decided to enlarge Lawrence Hall instead, with a special room at the south end for Chapin's collection. There would also be a skylit reading room and various seminar rooms, the whole to cost about $100,000.

Harding & Seaver's plans were in hand at the start of 1917, when Amherst College began building its own new library, an up-to-date Georgian Revival building by McKim, Mead & White. This changed matters. It scarcely seemed worth investing the $80,000 to $100,000 that Harding's addition would cost, when the enlarged building would still be outclassed by Amherst's library. And so in 1919 Garfield went back to Cram and asked him to tackle the library problem afresh.

Cram's task was complicated by the need to satisfy both Stetson and Chapin and also by the siting. Should the main facade address itself to Main Street, as Williams buildings traditionally did, or should it face Chapin Hall and establish a new formal axis between the two buildings devoted to the humanities? Cram's solution was a building with two formal facades—a main facade on the west and another, equally stately one to the south. This led to locating the Chapin collection upstairs—approached by a staircase of baronial splendor. As for the library's main reading room, this Cram placed on the north side, so as to avoid direct light (apparent from outside by its blank walls). Finally, he swiveled the bookstack out to the east, where the ground dropped and where there was ample room for future extensions.

The library's twin facades show Cram's versatility. Chapin Hall was imposing but rather humorless; his Stetson Library, by contrast, strikes a

The Library Quad: (from left) Hollander Hall, Stetson Library, Schapiro Hall

Stetson Library, Reading Room

note of welcome. It answers Chapin's projecting portico with a deeply recessed loggia, suggestive of shelter and receptiveness. The arcaded central section is flanked by two bold projecting blocks that serve as bookends, so to speak, and establish a lively play of solids and voids, something that Cram, a champion of the Gothic, obviously enjoyed.

Stetson Library was a central component of President Garfield's vision of the progressive college and its civilizing mission. To express that mission poetically, the names of ten authors would be incised on the facades, a kind of symbolic card catalog of Western civilization. The list was debated heatedly, and two early choices were crossed out. One was Ralph Waldo Emerson, who was prevented from lecturing at the college over half a century earlier because of his heretical freethinking and who was still persona non grata. (He was replaced by Benjamin Franklin.) Francis Bacon, who may have seemed too obscure, was replaced by Shakespeare. That name was too long for a lapidary inscription, and so as a compromise the Elizabethan *Shakespere* was used, giving rise to the tired joke that Williams is very stingy in awarding an A.

The interior contains two superb public spaces, the original reading room and the Chapin Library. The reading room is of a piece with the facade, expressing the same sort of gentlemanly ease that one expects from a London club. But the Chapin Library is something else again. A two-story space, surrounded by a gallery and crowned by a shallow segmental vault, it is purely neoclassical. Unlike the hearty Georgian detail elsewhere in the building, it is Robert and James Adam who provide the inspiration for the delicate pastel colors and slender, graceful ornament. (See p. 4, opposite the dedication page.)

Cram designed his stacks for future enlargement, and in 1956 Cram & Ferguson (the principals long dead) returned to double the capacity with a $400,000 addition that replicated the original design in somewhat simpler form. But this too was outpaced by the constant arrival of about 12,000 books each year, the rate always increasing. By 1970 the library held about 365,000 volumes, and it reached about a million in 1990, a number that could not be accommodated simply by building addition upon addition; a new library was desperately needed.

Sawyer followed Lawrence and Stetson as the college's third purpose-built library. (See p. 48.) It was the work of Ben Weese, a talented Chicago architect, whose design expressed three basic ideas. First was the notion that book reading and book storage should no longer be separated as at the original Sawyer, where bookstacks and reading carrels were freely mixed in within an open plan. Second was that the furniture should be as informal as possible, as cozy and inhabitable as a tree house, culminating in a burrowlike carrel train, instantly renamed by the students as the "monkey carrels." (Much of the furniture was designed by his wife, Cynthia.) The third was Weese's response to a chronic problem of postwar college libraries, typically placed at the center of their campuses but with a single entrance (necessary for security) that formed an insurmountable obstacle to pedestrian traffic. Weese had the sharp idea of running a passage directly through his building, placing the entrance in the middle rather than on the periphery. The library opened in 1973, at which point the redundant stacks of Stetson Library were turned into faculty offices (with Hobbit-scaled low ceilings).

four man reading table section through carrel train

carrel train/lower level

The furniture at Sawyer was to be as informal and cozy as possible, which was a fairly new idea in library design. And nothing could be cozier than the famous "monkey carrels" designed by Cynthia Weese—a blend of tree house and space capsule that could only have happened in 1970.

Sawyer Library, main stair facing east

Like Cram before him, Weese designed his library with an eye toward future expansion, and he left a terrace to the north where an addition could be built. But by 2003, when that addition became necessary, there was an unexpected complication. The shelves in Sawyer were twenty-three inches apart, too narrow for the wheelchair accessibility that the Americans with Disabilities Act required. The building committee did the math and discovered that to build an addition would produce a larger library that held fewer books. Had it not been for new codes that were unanticipated when Sawyer was built thirty years earlier, it would have been enlarged to the north as Weese had envisioned.

Five architectural firms were interviewed, and four of them brought schematic proposals for a new library. Only Peter Bohlin of BCJ Architects did not, suggesting instead that he would offer alternatives at each stage, letting the clients participate more actively in the design process. His low-key approach pleased the building committee, but he had another key credential: in 1997 he had designed the house of Bill Gates, the founder of Microsoft. In the new library, computer technology was to play a significant role; the commission went to Bohlin's firm.

The plan was costly, but it had one great appeal: the removal of Sawyer opened up a grand axis parallel to Main Street, running all the way from the facade of Stetson, past Chapin and Paresky, to the new '62 Center. Here a generous public concourse would connect the humanities and form a humane alternative to the automobile spine of Main Street. In fact, Denise Scott Brown—the noted Philadelphia planner—had strongly recommended the creation of just such an axis in her 2002 proposal for the Williams campus plan. Bohlin's inspiration was to carry that axis directly through the building and to set a final, unexpected emphasis at its east end.

The new library was grafted onto the original Stetson to form a surprising spatial sequence. The visitor, having traversed the long axis leading from Paresky, first encountered the regal Georgian frontispiece of the old library. Next followed the dark wainscoted lobby, a space of compression, after which came the startling spatial release of the new lobby, a soaring space housed in the

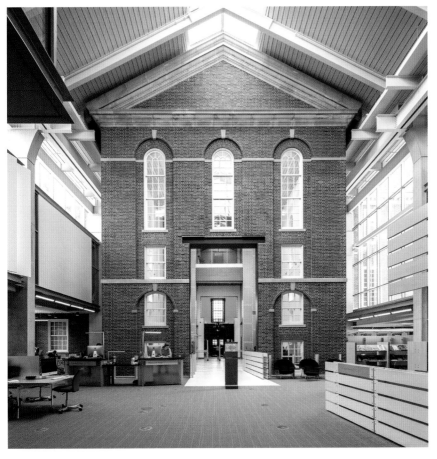

TOP Sawyer Library is entered through what was once the bookstack of Stetson.
BOTTOM Sawyer Library, east face at night

shell of Cram's stacks. Finally, the procession culminates where the forward axis of the old building meets the cross axis of the new one. Here the ground drops away, as the visitor discovers that the library's entire east wall is five stories of glass and that the passage has been one from darkness to light—a fitting metaphor for a library.

Bohlin corrected one of the glaring faults of Sawyer Library, whose free-flowing interior and open plan did not work as well as intended. Bit by bit, its open spaces had been appropriated by various branches of the expanding library administration. Restoring the clear distinction between reading books and storing books, Bohlin placed the stacks to the north and the reading areas to the south—a lucid division of function that comes into focus once the visitor reaches the central stair. (Alas, a stair that is just a bit too narrow and steep for its location, although in compensation it was built out of marble salvaged from the demolished stacks.)

Bohlin deliberately gave each face of the new library its distinct material, rhythm, and color: glass for the east wall, red brick for the south, and Vermont green slate for the west—so as to form a pleasant color contrast with the red brick of Stetson. Had all four sides of the new library been of the same material, it would have read as a more massive object and tended to overpower the original Stetson. In Bohlin's hybrid, now reborn as Stetson–Sawyer Library, we do not have one building stuck on another but a building transforming itself step by step into another, emerging from its brick chrysalis to become a shimmering wall of light. If it lacks the fully resolved aesthetic unity that marked its three predecessors, it is because that was never its goal.

At an early stage of the design process, David Pilachowski, director of libraries, made the programmatic decision that the building would "give primacy to people space and not collections." This had sweeping consequences for the plan. The amount of space devoted to book storage was reduced through the use of compact shelving and offsite storage. And this in turn freed a great deal of space for students to collaborate on group projects, something for which there was constantly increasing demand. Sawyer devoted only two rooms to such, the new library twenty. The outcome was a building with a different social character from its predecessors. If the earlier Williams libraries had something of the solemnity of the chapel, the new one has a conviviality not unlike that of the student center—and is truer to the nature of the student experience today.

47 Class of 1966 Environmental Center
Kellogg House, 1790s; Addition: Black River Design Architects, 2010–15

In 1967 Williams under President Jack Sawyer opened the first Center for Environmental Studies in a small liberal arts college. Initially located inside the Van Rensselaer House, then in Kellogg House after Sawyer Library replaced the former, the center has grown in importance over the years. Like many an old Williamstown building, Kellogg has wandered around town. Originally, the chestnut-framed house stood on Main Street on the present site of Hopkins Hall, where it served for many years as the house of the college president. The first move, to the north, was to a place from which the construction of Stetson forced a second move, even farther to the north. For sentimental and philosophical reasons, the staff of the center wanted to preserve this fine example of early Williamstown domestic architecture, and it was once more picked up and transported. On the new site, north and slightly west of the library, Kellogg is joined by a three-story addition that takes advantage of the slope of the site to appear to be the same height as its predecessor. The designer was John Rahill (Class of 1968), of Black River Design Architects.

Dedicated in 2015, the center earned Petal Status Certification in 2017 for meeting six of the seven standards for the Living Building Challenge, the ultimate worldwide level of achievement for architecture that uses materials safe for humans and the environment. At that date, only eleven buildings in the world had met all seven environmental performance criteria; the solar panels at Williams failed by about 20 percent to come up to their expected level of production. From the beginning, the building itself was planned as a teaching tool. Its rainwater catchment and treatment system was the first in Massachusetts, for instance, and subsequent buildings in the state have been able to profit from the experience of the Williams system—although it turned

out to have problems with groundwater infiltration. Because the project was so far in front of the sustainable building movement, the parts had to be cobbled together, each element of the ensemble an experiment in its own right.

Outside, 35 percent of the site is devoted to agriculture, one requirement for certification. To the south are orchards, to the north beds for berries and vegetables. Originally storm runoff was to be returned directly to the ground in storm gardens, as it is in front of Hollander, but the unexpectedly high water table of the site forced the creation of ponds, now inhabited by frogs that control the mosquito population. The large pieces of stone that surround the patio at the entrance are the piers of old bridges, scrubbed clean of barnacles that proved dangerously sharp. Inside one finds the ultimate use of local materials: wood paneling milled locally from trees cleared from the site, as well as slates reused from the demolition of the stacks of the Stetson Library next door.

Kellogg House, restored and with solar panels on its roof, is now the west wing, which is entered in the center under a pergola that supports solar panels. The Black River part of the design includes the entrance area and the three-story eastern wing, painted white like the old house. But the wing is completely contemporary in form, with a roof raked in a single plane and solar screening hung from metal posts that stand free of the facade to resemble an Erector Set. It is never easy to bring something totally new in form into harmony with something old, and it is not clear that success was achieved. If that is debatable for the south side, the north can fairly be labeled unsuccessful. What is clear is that the primary purpose of the structure as a teaching device has been well met.

48   Dodd House

Unknown architect, ca. 1869; North wing addition, 1902; Parsons House addition, 1915

The land abutting Mission Park was prime real estate for Williams College professors, and those who could afford it built themselves comfortable houses. One was that of Cyrus Morris Dodd, who graduated in 1855 from Williams, where he taught mathematics until his death in 1897. Although one student recalled it as a "somewhat somber house, apart from others," Dodd himself was anything but somber. A kind, humorous man, known affectionately to students as Tommy Dodd, he was famous for interrupting his lectures to recite long passages of memorized Latin poetry. So often did he do this that the campus legend arose that he set out to write a grammar of Latin and that when the manuscript was destroyed in a fire, he was at such a loss that he became a professor of mathematics.

Following Dodd's death, his daughters, Grace and Agnes, enlarged the house and converted it into a twenty-room boardinghouse called Netherleigh. In 1909 they sold it to a group of alumni known as the Williams Alumni House,

In good Victorian eclectic fashion, the house of Cyrus Morris Dodd meandered playfully, offering playful bits of incident in its dormers, balconies, and chimneys. As with virtually every house in nineteenth-century Williamstown, its architect is unknown.

Inc., who wished to provide "a suitable place of social entertainment for the stockholders, alumni, president, and trustees of Williams College and their guests." In 1956 it was acquired by the college, which undertook a $250,000 remodeling in 1960 that gave it distinctive picture windows on the east side. For most of its history it was known as the Williams Inn, a name it retained until 1974, when it became a dormitory after the completion of a new Williams Inn; it was then renamed Dodd House. Until the building of Paresky, it had one of the most popular student dining halls; it is now used only for special occasions. After the building's countless enlargements and alterations, the discerning visitor can still spot features dating to the days when Professor Dodd would invite his wayward students to drop by for a kindly chat.

49 Mission Park and the *Haystack Monument*
Harvey Rice and Berkshire Marble Company, 1866–67

Mission Park is an ambiguous designation at Williams; while it generally refers to the modern dormitory, there is a park of that name that existed for more than a century before the dorm was built. Although it is not demarcated in any apparent way, it is a specific area with a clear status in Massachusetts law, which has led to a rather curious administrative relationship between the state and the college.

At the beginning of the nineteenth century the Williams campus was not nearly as extensive as it is today. At that time virtually all the land north of Main Street was private property, part of it known as Sloan's Meadow. In 1806 a spot in that area was the site of one of the most significant moments in college history.

In that year, five students preparing to be Congregationalist ministers were holding an outdoor prayer meeting in the meadow when they were caught in a sudden rainstorm and took shelter under a haystack. Exhilaration seems to have led to inspiration, and the students vowed to commit themselves to Christian missionary activity and "to spread the good news" of the Bible through the world, that is, to preach the gospel.

This was the famous Haystack Meeting, which led to the creation of the American Board of Commissioners for Foreign Missions. The first mission inspired by the Haystack Meeting was to India in 1812, followed by others to the Near East (1819), China (1830), and Africa (1833). The Commissioners for Foreign Missions did more than merely proselytize; they also worked to create schools, hospitals, and orphanages. In the United States they campaigned vigorously against forced Native American removal. Some of their most important accomplishments were indirect: in the process of translating the Bible, they codified some eighteen languages that until that point had only existed in spoken form. In terms of reach and scope, the American Foreign Missions was one of the most consequential social movements of the past two centuries.

For nearly half a century after the meeting, the meadow remained in private hands, the place where the haystack had stood marked only by a cedar stake in the ground. Then, in 1855, Charles Stoddard bought for $2,500 a ten-acre rectangular plot, bordered by Park Street on the west, running north nearly to what is now Lynde Lane, east to what would become the west edge of the college cemetery, and south to an east–west line that begins at the south side of the entry to Mission Park Drive on Park Street. Stoddard's intention was to secure the land for the college, and four years later, for $100, he transferred it to the Mission Park Association, which was incorporated by the Massachusetts legislature with Stoddard, Mark Hopkins, and Albert Hopkins as the principal officers. With the Hopkins brothers in that role, the park was effectively, if not yet legally, under the college's control. In the act of incorporation the association was described as being for "erecting and placing…suitable monuments and other memorials to commemorate the origin and progress of American missions." This remains the official purpose of the park, for when it was transferred to the college in 1885, the college assumed those duties, a necessary condition in order for the land to remain tax-free.

In 1866 the site of the Haystack Meeting was still marked only by a stake, but in that year Harvey Rice (Class of 1824), an influential Cleveland newspaperman and politician, struck by the contrast between that and the newly erected marble monuments to Presidents Ebenezer Fitch and Edward Dorr Griffin in the college cemetery, decided that something similar should be placed at the Haystack site. His first design was dreadful—"built of gray sandstone, so as to resemble...a veritable haystack"—and President Hopkins told him so. In his second proposal, he aimed to make something "more strictly emblematical, and to combine the historical with the classical."

As conceived by Rice, the *Haystack Monument* is a tapered marble stele topped by a three-foot globe; on its face is carved a representation of the original haystack, looking very much like a beehive. Along with the names of the five students at the original Haystack Meeting is the emblematic inscription "The Field is the World." The meaning is clear: from the modest seed of the haystack in a field, the movement has sprouted to cover the whole world. The monument was dedicated on July 28, 1867, with an address by Rice, who praised it as "strictly a Berkshire production, composed of Berkshire marble quarried at Alford, and wrought in the workshops of The Berkshire Marble Company."

The *Haystack Monument*, besides its symbolic meaning, is a significant document of the history of Williams. It reminds us that the college's religious mission touched much of the world—even as late as 1868 one-third of the graduates went on to be ordained. Nothing else on campus testifies so eloquently that Williams was once better known for its ministers than its bankers.

If the materials and workmanship of the monument were emphatically local, the landscaping around it was rather self-consciously not. Although there are no records that state it clearly,

the evidence of the plantings suggests that the choice of trees was made to refer to the international character of the missionary activities, as there are, among others, a Japanese umbrella tree, horse chestnut, ginkgo, Norway spruce and maple, and a hinoki false cypress. It is not unreasonable to imagine that some foreign trees were brought back by missionaries to be planted at the spot where it all began, but as yet no proof of that has been found.

50   Williams College Cemetery
1858

Cemeteries that serve specialized populations are distinctive in character. The Williams College Cemetery has a charming and unexpected unity. It contains a great many distinctive markers—strong individual personalities each making strongly personal statements—and yet the entirety has an unmistakable sense of gregarious community.

Soon after the land that became Mission Park was purchased in 1855, Professor Arthur Latham Perry had the idea of setting aside a small part of it as a college cemetery. (Up to that point, residents of Williamstown ended up in the burying ground of the Congregational meetinghouse.) He took his plan to President Mark Hopkins, who, to Perry's dismay, "took no interest in the scheme, and at once discarded it." Perry, on his way to becoming the country's most important economist, was not easily rebuffed and turned to "the next most influential person on the premises," as he described Professor Albert Hopkins, the president's brother. This Hopkins did indeed have the clout to establish the cemetery, although it was not placed on the newly acquired park but just beyond its eastern border. Perry's victory over Mark Hopkins was bittersweet: the very first body to be laid in the cemetery turned out to be that of Gray Perry, his firstborn son.

Cemeteries do not become prestigious until they have acquired a certain number of respected bodies. This takes time, but one way to speed up the process was to acquire them from other cemeteries—a practice strange to us but common in the nineteenth century. It was the great coup of Williams College to secure the return of the body of its first president. President Fitch was reinterred in 1864, but when it proved impossible to return the body of Griffin, his successor, a cenotaph was instead raised in 1865. Each man is honored with a stately, fourteen-foot marble monument of similar but not identical form: an urn above a mighty tapered stele. (The point seems to have been that these were different men but of equal dignity.) Their place of honor at the center of the cemetery gives it a poignant symbolic order, that of an eternal faculty meeting across the generations, feisty but silent. President Griffin's monument was carved by Logan, Fuller & Co., and presumably President Fitch's was as well.

Logan, Fuller & Co. and the firm of Linn & Mead (which made the somber monument to Edward Lasell) were both of Pittsfield, and they were responsible

for nearly all the early markers. These were invariably of Berkshire marble, but despite the similarity in materials and workmanship, there is a considerable variety in expression. Isaac Newton Lincoln, who in 1862 was the first professor to be buried in the cemetery, established the precedent that a tomb might say something about the professor's subject matter. He taught Latin and French, and his tomb is a classical allegory of opened books and inverted urns. Charles Franklin Gilson, who taught German, placed a suitably melancholy inscription beneath his neo-Grec cross: *Meine Trübsal ist mein Glück* ("My gloom is my good fortune"). Both are on the south side of the cemetery, as is the granite-fronted mausoleum of President Paul Chadbourne.

Nearby is Mark Hopkins's grave, which is marked by a bold table tomb—a granite slab carried on six rugged columns, which shows the widening variety of materials and tombstone types at the end of the nineteenth century. Also in the vicinity is the handsome Celtic cross of his son, Amos Lawrence Hopkins. The visitor should not neglect the other side of the cemetery. In the northeast corner is a poignant cluster of monuments to Williams students who died before graduation. Finally, before leaving, one should seek out the art historian S. Lane Faison Jr. and inspect the back of his stone, just above ground level, where he extends a characteristically whimsical greeting to passers-by.

51　Mission Park Dormitory
Mitchell-Giurgola Associates, 1971; Renovations: Centerline, 2002–4

The second of the great dormitory complexes built during the Jack Sawyer presidency is Mission Park Dormitory, the angular, gray concrete wall that marks the northern edge of the central part of the campus, downslope from the *Haystack Monument*. Sawyer chose an architect, Romaldo Giurgola, who had little experience working on college campuses, but he was the dean of the architecture school at Columbia, an important center for training future architects in contemporary design. In 2000 Giurgola moved to Australia, where he won the competition to design the new national capitol building at Canberra. Sawyer explained his decision to give the work to someone other than Benjamin Thompson by saying that he did not think that all the new college buildings should look as if they "came from the same cookie cutter."

The name Mission Park was proposed by Sawyer to make it easier to get permission from the state to intrude slightly (less than 5 percent) on the inviolable confines of the park that had been established with the incorporation of the Mission Park Association in 1859, and the choice of names for parts of the complex may well have been made to be consistent with the memorial designation of the land.

The building's height was fixed so that the view of the mountains to the north from the upslope entrance to the park on the south would not be blocked. The desire to temper the elongated bulk of the building resulted in breaking it into four separate residential "houses" named for alumni, two of whom played important roles in attempting to ameliorate the effects of slavery in the American South. Samuel J. Mills (Class of 1809), a founder of the American Board of Commissioners for Foreign Missions, died at sea returning from a trip to Africa to found a mission in a free state established for ex-slaves. Samuel Chapman Armstrong (Class of 1862) founded the Hampton Institute after the Civil War, in which he had commanded African American troops.

In the earliest plans, the four houses were to be served by four separate dining halls. The independent dining rooms would be connected, two to a side, to a spine, or corridor, running upslope from the dormitories into Mission Park. This lovely concept to retain the intimacy of student housing and dining units would have broken the budget. It would also have run afoul of the Commonwealth of Massachusetts, which guarded the boundaries of Mission Park. Giurgola's design would have extended crab-like claws into the park, in a gesture that forcefully recalls the crustacean-like shapes of Michelangelo's fortification drawings of the 1520s for his native Florence. Giurgola's Italian heritage played a significant role in his version of radically contemporary architecture. Instead of adhering to the scheme presented in the model, dining was ultimately concentrated in a single trapezoidal space on the building's

Mission Park Dormitory,
model of early project

south side, with enormous glass walls facing the landscape.

As originally built, the building offered an extraordinary experience of a kinetic architectural inversion. Students returning to the building for a meal would descend the hillside of the park and enter the building through a single door that led into a tight corridor flanked by the blank walls of two lounges. Beyond the lounges they would descend a broad, skylit staircase to the lower level, turn left into the low-ceilinged food-service area, emerge under the floor of the lounges to get drinks, then move into the surprisingly tall, expansive space of the dining area, whose glass walls, opening onto the park, made the interior seem to be outdoors. On their exterior the lounges appeared to be a single building, closely resembling Le

Corbusier's Villa Savoye raised on pilotis, standing in the "exterior" space of the dining room.

A thoughtless renovation of 2002–4 by Centerline wrecked this experience, certainly the most sophisticated architectural promenade Williams ever enjoyed. The detailing of parts of the renovation is shockingly unsympathetic to the style of the original: shiny, natural-wood crown moldings in a pure machine-age interior. One original detail of the delightful inside-outside game Giurgola played survives in the western corner of the dining hall, where the rounded facade of the house within the house punches through the glass wall to become an actual exterior.

The planned four residential houses were fused into one V-shaped mass pointing north, with the eastern wing taller and the western shorter to respond to the slope of the land. Students are convinced that the building was laid out to resemble an eagle in flight. The design, highly sculptural with sharp angles, vigorous diagonals, and an occasional round tower, falls into the category of what Gerhard Kallmann, the architect of Boston City Hall, dubbed "Action Architecture." Outside, the whole restless mass is faced with precast concrete panels. Inside, unrelieved gray concrete staircases had the bleakness and anomie of contemporary Michelangelo Antonioni films, and the rooms are so irregularly shaped that students find it frustratingly impossible to arrange the furniture in more than one way. Strict Massachusetts fire codes forced the claustrophobic enclosure of the open living rooms that each suite was meant to enjoy.

52   Thompson Infirmary
Allen & Collens, 1909–10

Williams College established its infirmary in the 1890s, acquiring and enlarging an old house on Park Street. Although it was "a modern hospital [with] thirteen of the best trained nurses," President Hopkins wanted something less provisional. In his 1905 annual report, he declared that the college was in urgent need of "a substantial, permanent, and fire-proof infirmary, amply endowed." This is the sort of statement meant to catch the attention of a donor, who appeared in 1909 in the form of Mrs. Frederick Ferris Thompson. Her donation of $68,000 to build and equip the infirmary would be the last of the great Thompson bequests. Like all of them, it was executed by the family architects, Allen & Collens.

By now the design work was firmly in the hands of the junior partner, Charles Collens, who had just finished designing Fitch Hall, another Colonial Revival building. But here different considerations were at play: the infirmary had to be sober and dignified enough to inspire confidence but also reassuringly domestic in character, so as to comfort a sick student far from home. And some of those students needed comforting: the infirmary

had an operating room in the northeast corner and was perfectly capable of performing an appendectomy—especially in the days when it was staffed by doctors who had served on the World War I battlefield.

53   Torrance Hunt Tennis Center and Chaffee Tennis House
Chris Williams, 1993

Set at an angle at the intersection of Stetson Road and Lynde Lane, the building is a clever New England adaptation of the southern "dog trot" house, with two masses separated by an open area covered by its own roof. One side holds male and female locker rooms, the other a display of trophies. The simple, square pavilions with pyramidal roofs distantly echo Louis I. Kahn's noble Trenton Jewish Community Center Bath House (1955). Beyond the building is an ample terrace that overlooks six hard courts and provides a spectacular view of

Lindsay S. Morehouse Memorial

Pine Cobble Mountain. Passing through the space of the dog trot to the terrace nicely sets up the view.

The Chaffee Tennis House is named for a legendary figure, Clarence Chaffee, who coached tennis, squash, and soccer for thirty-two years. Between ages seventy and eighty-six, he won fifty national senior tennis titles, and five months after a heart attack at eighty he won all four national eighty-plus singles titles.

At the south entrance to the tennis courts is a memorial to Lindsay S. Morehouse (Class of 2000), the tennis team captain who was the youngest graduate of Williams College to lose her life in the attacks of September 11, 2001. Set between a pair of thornless honeysuckle trees (*Gleditsia triacanthos*), it is fittingly quiet and gentle.

54   Stetson Apartments ("Poker Flats")

Kenneth Reynolds, 1946; Conversion to student apartments, Einhorn Yaffee Prescott, 1993

Young faculty returning from World War II, now with families, desperately needed housing. The twelve two-bedroom units of the Stetson Apartments were the answer. In a rush to get something built, Kenneth Reynolds (Class of 1916) quickly produced a long, dull, two-story brick building with tiny porches protecting the entrances on the north side. Erected on an empty field north of the campus, the apartments seemed so far away from the center of the college that the inhabitants dubbed them "Poker Flats," as in the Outcast thereof. A new technology of precast concrete beams, called flexicord, allowed for rapid construction. The beams simultaneously formed the ceilings of the apartments below and the floors of those above. They turned out to be extraordinarily good at transmitting sound.

Whatever Poker Flats may lack in architectural liveliness is made up for by its setting. It has for a backyard the most beautiful meadow at Williams, which is edged on the east side with stately red oaks that were among the

four hundred planted by Francis Lynde Stetson in 1912—surely one of the greatest gifts ever made to the college.

The desire of small groups of students to keep house for themselves led to the renovation of Poker Flats as student apartments. Einhorn Yaffee Prescott, an Albany firm, greatly enlivened the exterior by adding elaborate porches and staircases on both the north and south sides that give the building a much grander sense of scale, as well as some useful outdoor spaces.

55 Cole Field House
Densmore, Le Clear & Robbins, 1925

> The Field house situated on Stetson road will have locker accommodations for all the students of the college and teams competing in Williamstown and will relieve considerably the present congestion in Lasell.
> —*North Adams Transcript* (May 11, 1926)

For decorous academic buildings President Garfield turned to Cram & Ferguson, but when it came to gyms and power plants, he wanted sensible technicians. He favored Densmore, Le Clear & Robbins, an architecture-engineering firm founded by three Harvard graduates. In 1922 they drew up plans for a massive gym on Cole Field. But two years of effort raised only a fraction of the necessary funds. President Garfield decided to build what he could afford: a small central block with showers and lockers. The rest of the building would follow as funds came in. But it was soon clear that this was unlikely; in 1926 the trustees decided to cut their losses and to enlarge Lasell Gym instead.

This history explains the most unusual aspect of the field house, its curiously detached site, waiting for the addition that never came. Nonetheless, Edward Densmore must have guessed that his building would remain an incomplete fragment, and so he worked hard to make a building that could stand alone and still make a stately and dignified impression. It is nowhere near as ornate as Cram's buildings, but then Densmore did not have Cram's budget. Every inch of space had to be exploited: even the attic was used by members of visiting teams as sleeping quarters during the early years of the building.

Just behind the field house the terrain slopes down to a pond; beyond it lie two long playing fields that boast spectacular views of the hills rising on the north to the Vermont border. Cole Field is one of glories of the Williams campus and contributes greatly to its special character, celebrated in "The Mountains," the college alma mater that refers to mountains rising with their "kingly forest robes."

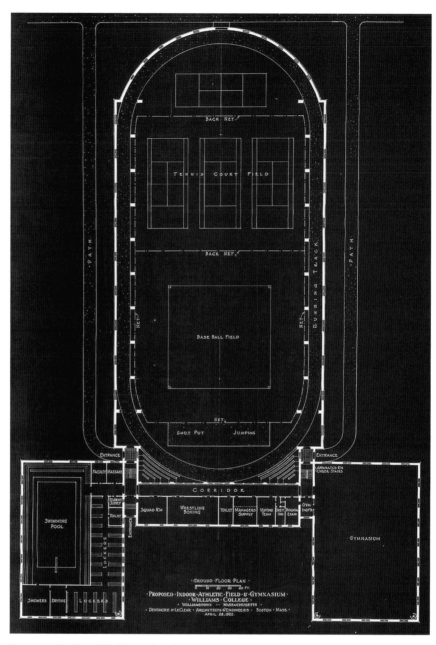

Densmore, Le Clear & Robbins, plan of proposed gymnasium, 1922

TOP **Cole Field House** BOTTOM **Cole Field, view looking north from Cole Field House**

56 Tyler House (Psi Upsilon)
Andrews, Jones, Biscoe and Whitmore, 1927; Annex: Unitec Inc., Lindstrom and Associates, 1972

Tyler House is the most remote dormitory on campus; students who live there sometimes call it Siberia. That is because the fraternity that built it, Psi Upsilon, came late to Williams College, in 1913, by which time the prime real estate on Fraternity Row had already been claimed. Forced to look elsewhere, it made a virtue of necessity. It found a picturesque hillside site near Park Street, a setting that suggested a freer and looser treatment than the symmetrical clubhouses on Main Street, standing in parade dress. Accordingly, Psi Upsilon built a low, rambling affair, 175 feet long, of red brick and a roof of green slate. The fraternity did not conceal that its primary desire was to be fashionable, at least according to the dictates of 1925: "The English style represented in the new home has been recognized as the most desirable for chapter houses and throughout the country the colleges are choosing the traditional Tudor architecture for prospective houses."

Unlike any of the other former fraternity houses on campus, Tyler is not entered from the front but from the side, the part of the house that faces the long driveway. Its plan was hardly Tudor: the large reception room opened onto a library on one side and a card room on the other, giving students a choice of work or play. To make the dining room suitable for dance parties, it was "specially designed with a large octagonal bay to accommodate an orchestra." The architects were Andrews, Jones, Biscoe & Whitmore, a Boston firm specializing in academic buildings; J. R. Hampson & Co., of Pittsfield, was the contractor for the lucrative project, which, according to the fraternity, cost

$150,000. Luxury is not cheap: Williams Hall, a much larger building, cost only $124,000.

In 1972 an annex was built, curving away from the original fraternity and down the driveway that connects the students to Park Street and the Mission Park Dormitory, where they eat, and to the distant campus. Recognizing that even Siberia needs to be made livable, the college went out of its way to make the annex comfortable, giving it forty singles arranged in suites so that every two rooms share a bath. It is simple and unadorned, and not at all discordant with the old frat house.

The visitor should view Tyler House and Mears House in succession, two designs of 1925 that solve the same architectural problem in formal and informal terms.

ENDNOTE

1 "The Mark Hopkins Memorial," *Fitchburg Sentinel,* December 28, 1887, 4.

Northwest Quadrant

57   Sloan House (President's House)
Architect unknown, 1801

Samuel Sloan, an early settler of Williamstown, arrived from Connecticut as a blacksmith, but shrewd investments in real estate made him one of the richest men in the early history of the town. Although his holdings were largely in South Williamstown and Hancock, he was determined to make his presence known in the town's northern reaches, where the central buildings of the community— meetinghouse and the college—had been recently erected. He acquired an original lot across the street from West College, dismantled the house already there and moved it to South Street, and then erected his own mansion, the most architecturally sophisticated structure, with the most beautifully carved ornament, in the whole village. It is highly unlikely that carvers with such skill and such knowledge of classical and contemporary precedents were local. The ornamental parts of the facade must have been produced elsewhere and shipped, with some difficulty, to Williamstown. Salem, Massachusetts, graced with houses by Samuel McIntire, is a likely source. The facade is of a quality that deserves a far more detailed analysis than any other building in this guide receives.

Although the two-story, white clapboard facade is broader than it is tall, the proportions of the articulating elements are much elongated. The five bays are separated by Ionic pilasters whose proportions are far more slender than those of the Greek Ionic order. Each pilaster supports the vestige of an architrave and frieze that holds up a continuous cornice. No classical architect would have so deliberately compromised crucial elements of an order. Whoever designed this house intentionally sacrificed a continuous entablature in order to make room for the tops of the second-story windows, whose height increased sunlight in the south-facing interior. The vertical thrust of the pilasters continues through the cornice into the chunky piers of the balustrade that support vases with tops that pierce the air. This is a trick that goes back to the sixteenth century, to the work of Michelangelo and Palladio, but filtered through the attenuated elegance of the contemporary work of Robert Adam in England.

The central bay of the facade is wider, serving to stress the front door and the central hall behind it. The door, with its round-arched fanlight, is flanked by pairs of Ionic half columns that frame sidelights and hold up an entablature whose frieze echoes the triglyph-like vertical patterns and two-handled vases that appear in the fragmented entablature of the large order of the facade. The tops of the half columns are at the same level as those of the ground-floor windows. Above this order rests a rectangular panel, also subdivided into three parts, that reaches the same height as the bottoms of the upper windows. Over this panel rises a tripartite Palladian window, or Serliana, whose Ionic pilasters and round-arched central element play a game of theme and variation with the parts of the door below.

Above this extraordinary doorway, in the center of the balustrade, is a panel that sports a relief of two hearts joined by a chain. It is often said that Sloan built this house as a wedding present for his daughter, on whose marriage the relief would have made a sardonic comment. That story appears to be apocryphal. Sloan had five daughters. Would one have been singled out for such largesse? Actually, Sloan lived in the house himself with his wife. His was one of the chained hearts. After Sloan's death in 1815, his only son, Douglas, occupied the house with his widowed mother until her death in 1828. At that point Douglas moved to upstate New York.

In 1858 the house was donated to the college by Nathan Jackson, a relative of Ephraim Williams and a frequent donor, to be used as a house for its presidents. It served in that capacity until the presidency of Harry Payne, only to be reoccupied by Morty Schapiro and again abandoned by Adam Falk. To the rear, on the north side, is a large addition of the early twentieth century that makes more room for entertainment on the first floor and private family quarters and guest rooms above. Noise from increasing truck traffic climbing the hill on Main Street has made the building unpleasant for family occupancy.

The strangely vacant lot to the west of the house on Main Street, a prime piece of real estate, once held the brick Williamstown Academy, which was acquired and then replaced by St. Patrick's Roman Catholic Church in 1879. That brick Gothic church, visible in the Lucien R. Burleigh lithograph of 1889, stood only until 1896, when a new priest, perhaps not entirely legally, sold the property to Williams College, which razed it. (See p. 26.) St. Patrick's new sanctuary on Southworth Street was dedicated in 1897. For the once-staunchly Congregationalist college, the presence of a sizable Roman Catholic Church right next to the President's House and across the street from the college's original building created a serious problem of symbolism.

58 First Congregational Church

Joseph R. Richards and Charles T. Rathbun, 1866; Renovation: Charles Crothers Grant, 1914

At the very center of the Williams campus is a building that does not belong to the college: the white clapboard First Congregational Church with its slender Ionic portico and soaring steeple. This building of 1914 replicates the Congregationalist Church in Old Lyme, Connecticut, of 1816, which in turn is based on eighteenth-century English prototypes, particularly James Gibbs's St. Martin in the Fields (1726), in London. And so the Williamstown church is a copy of a copy (albeit a splendid one), an architectural idea passed on across the centuries.

Williamstown's first and second Meeting Houses (1768 and 1798) stood on the town green, directly on axis with East Main Street. In 1859 the building of the new chapel at Williams College inspired the congregation to erect a new meetinghouse for itself. But, upon inspection, the original building was "found to be in so good a state of preservation that the project for a new building [was] given up." Well preserved, but alas not fireproof; seven years later the building fell victim to an overheated stovepipe. The loss affected the college, which had always used the meetinghouse for commencement exercises. To maintain that relationship,

The First Congregational Church of 1866 was never demolished. Its distressingly Germanic facade was removed and the present colonial facade draped around its walls. It is an odd thing to cover fireproof brick walls with wooden clapboards, but in the United States in 1914 (as at other times), image was everything.

and to make the location of commencement more convenient, the college offered a new site on East Main Street, at the head of Spring Street. This was a radical departure from New England precedents, which always placed the meetinghouse on the town green, and signaled how important the college had become to the town.

Even more radical was the architecture. The white classical meetinghouse gave way to a medievalizing essay with round arches, pilaster strips, and a pair of picturesquely mismatched spires—an American version of the synthetic German style known as the *Rundbogenstil* (literally, "round-arched style"), the same style introduced with Lawrence Hall. The drawings were provided by Joseph R. Richards, a Boston architect who had recently made plans for the college's Civil War memorial. Construction was supervised by Charles T. Rathbun, a prolific Pittsfield architect, and completed in 1869.

By 1914, after Williams College had committed itself wholeheartedly to the Colonial Revival, the brick meetinghouse was now decidedly unfashionable. It was also too big; the building of Chapin Hall meant that the meetinghouse no longer needed to hold the entire graduating class at commencement. Donors stepped forward in the form of Robert Cluett and his wife, Elizabeth, wealthy summer residents from nearby Troy, New York. To reconfigure the church into a vision of the colonial past, they engaged Charles Crothers Grant, a New York architect. Grant removed the two towers, clad the brick walls in clapboard, and added an extravagantly slender Ionic portico from which rises the central spire. He maintained the original round-arched shape of the nave windows, cleverly disguising their medievalizing verticality. Colonial nostalgia governed the interior as well, expressed in the "old-time high backed pews, each with its paneled doorway."[1]

Grant and the Cluetts gave Williamstown a handsome colonial past that the rude original settlement never actually enjoyed. There is something disconcerting about all this, if one begins to ask what may lie behind the nostalgia that the new design represents. The early twentieth century in the United States was characterized by mass immigration of mostly Catholic peoples from Italy, Germany, and eastern Europe. The churches they erected were largely medievalizing, round-arched masonry structures that came to symbolize the intrusion of so many poor and poorly educated people into the established Protestant society of New England. The remodeling of the Congregational Church can be seen as an anti-immigrant, anti-Catholic statement of a kind common in early twentieth-century America—an affirmation of the traditional Protestant values of Anglo-Saxon New England at a time of convulsive and alarming social change.

59   Paresky Student Center
Ennead Architects (formerly Polshek Partners), 2004–7

When Morty Schapiro became president in 2000, he was determined to raise Williams to the very top echelon of small liberal arts colleges, not just in intellectual terms, but also in terms of student life. At that moment, there was a national vogue for grand student centers, and Schapiro made it a top priority to provide one for Williams. The college had a student center, Baxter Hall, but it had in many ways been a failure from its inception and needed to be replaced. (See p. 46.) Schapiro in particular was impressed with the new student center at Middlebury; indeed, a joke went around that he suffered from Middlebury envy.

Polshek Partners, designers of the Rose Center for Earth and Space at the Museum of Natural History, New York, and the new entrance to the Brooklyn Museum, were chosen from a long list of distinguished firms that were interviewed by the building committee. From the moment the Polshek team, headed by Richard Olcott, was interviewed, they proposed two principal features of a new building, to be constructed on the site of a razed Baxter on the west side of the lawn fronting Chapin Hall. It would have a porch reminiscent of New England summer hotels, like the Equinox Hotel in Manchester, Vermont; and a central interior space like the rustic, woodsy great halls of the National Park hotels of the American West, such as those at Glacier, Yellowstone, and Yosemite. Throughout the design process, those concepts never changed. Williams historian Sheafe Satterthwaite pointed out the irony of their choice of architectural forms designed to serve transients.

Paresky, named for the major donor, David Paresky (Class of 1960), presents a long, low facade to the Chapin lawn, with a dramatically cantilevered roof sheltering its broad porch. The architects wanted to open the interior of the building to the campus. The roof works as a symbol of this desire. Originally, the roof was to be hung from its back edge from a horizontal truss, to look as if the plane of the front wall had been raised to reveal its innards. Nice idea, but structurally impossible, and the present solution of suspending the roof from the truss at a point closer to its middle came into play. Note the steel cables that anchor the rear corners of the roof to the ground.

The oval snack bar at the southeast corner evokes the old snack bar in the same position in Baxter, which was the one successful space in that building, one that had served the community as a whole to bring town and gown together. The top of the oval that rises above the roof is cut on a slant that recalls a similar detail of Le Corbusier's Assembly building in Chandigarh, India, of the early 1960s. The oval is rotated so that one long exterior wall faces the diagonal path that approaches the building from Spring Street. Students can watch for friends, or they can observe people they do not want to see and skedaddle before they arrive. The perhaps unwarranted surfeit of exterior materials includes brick and cast stone that match the colors and textures of Chapin, and the large window on the exterior of the snack bar repeats the proportions of Chapin's portico. The front edge of the roof is deliberately aligned with the horizontal cornices of Chapin and the dormitory Sage Hall to Chapin's west.

Budget cuts reduced the building from three to two stories. Since Paresky had to fit on the Baxter footprint, the reduction produced a crowded interior, especially at meal times. The big interior hall, which retains the name Baxter, looks more like a work of Alvar Aalto than a national park hotel, but it is handsomely detailed and well lit. In the interior of the snack bar, the geometry of the oval walls of brick-faced concrete collides with the rectilinear grid of the evenly spaced support system of the rest of the building. An amusing way to pass some time is to figure out how this works.

60   Chapin Hall

Cram, Goodhue & Ferguson, 1910–11

Chapin Hall is the result of an unusually happy collaboration between donor, client, and architect, each with a distinctive vision for the building. The wealthy lawyer Alfred C. Chapin (Class of 1869), who lost his wife, Grace, suddenly in 1908, wanted a memorial in her honor. President Harry Garfield wanted a new kind of college culture, where students and faculty could interact more freely and naturally. And the architect Ralph Adams Cram, for his part, wanted a new kind of architecture, where buildings did not stand alone but related to one another by means of gracious spaces, paths, and landscaping.

    Conducting the trio was Bentley Warren, the college's lawyer and the chairman of the trustees' building committee. Warren advised Garfield on architectural matters, and it was he who gave Chapin the shortlist of possible architects: George M. Harding, the college's house architect; Henry Bigelow of Boston, who designed Williamstown's Cluett House, now the Pine Cobble School; and Cram, who had just build a handsome Colonial Revival campus for Sweet Briar College. Chapin was happy to let Garfield pick the architect and make all the architectural decisions, with one condition: there should be "marble columns at the entrance." Garfield selected Cram.

    Chapin's gift of $150,000 was to be spent on "an auditorium for Commencement and other academic exercises" so that the graduating class no

longer had to squeeze into the Congregational Church. When Cram visited the campus in spring 1909, he recommended buying the site of the church, which he would replace with "a Gothic building somewhat in the proportions and style of Westminster Hall." This would be a Gothic pendant to Thompson Chapel, which would be even more attractive if Hopkins Hall were pushed back to make a courtyard. These were alarming suggestions, and when Warren heard them, he cautioned President Garfield about repeating them to Chapin.

While on campus Cram considered other sites for the auditorium, none of which suited the Gothic, and he therefore proposed to make two designs, depending on the site: one Gothic and one Georgian. Chapin continued to let others make his decisions; he announced that his daughters "warmly and unanimously" preferred the Georgian design with its pedimented portico and stately marble columns.

This was all that Cram needed to hear. In late July he began turning his "somewhat scholastic sketches into a carefully thought out type of Georgian architecture." The building was to be of a dull red brick, laid in Flemish bond, with trim of white marble. Its interior would paraphrase James Gibbs's Senate House

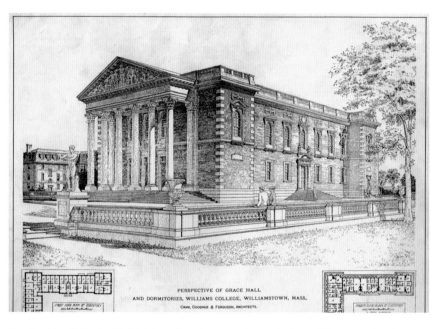

PERSPECTIVE OF GRACE HALL
AND DORMITORIES, WILLIAMS COLLEGE, WILLIAMSTOWN, MASS.
CRAM, GOODHUE & FERGUSON, ARCHITECTS.

President Garfield asked Ralph Adams Cram for attractive renderings of his proposed auditorium and dormitories to show them to trustees and possible donors. Cram told him curtly that "the making of show drawings is no part of an architect's duties" and that while he had twenty draftsmen working on the design of Chapin in 1910, not one of them was a professional illustrator. Fortunately, Garfield was willing to pay $150 to David A. Gregg, America's finest renderer, to make several appealing perspective drawings. Alas, the pedimental sculpture and ground-level balustrade were both casualties of cost overruns. (*Brickbuilder*, February 1911) at Cambridge University (1722–30), with its lower level of oak and plaster walls above the gallery level. As for the color scheme, McKim, Mead & White's recent Symphony Hall in Boston (1900) offered the best model: "low toned grays but with a good deal of gold worked into the decorative portions of the ceiling." The classical columns of the portico would be costly, and to shave $3,000 off his estimate, Cram recommended that each be built out of three separate drums rather than a single monolithic shaft. When Chapin heard this, he was vacationing in Paris, whose monolithic columns he had found time to admire. He instantly cabled back: monolithic columns were nonnegotiable.

When the site of Chapin, at the north end of a long axis proceeding from Main Street, was settled on later that summer, Garfield decided to add two dormitories to the program, which together would form a new quadrangle. Cram was immediately put to work. His renderings, three of which he later published, are remarkable for the attention they pay to the setting—his concern was not only to make buildings but to create a *place*, one of refinement and gentlemanly culture, suggesting thoughtful and unhurried conversations against a backdrop of sturdy tradition. The Olmsted brothers advised on the landscaping. The auditorium was to be approached "from the south by an avenue 100 feet wide with tall elms growing on either side," a translation of an ancient forum into the terms of a wooded American town.

Chapin was to get his monolithic columns, although not of marble. Each of the six Corinthian columns was carved from a single block of Indiana limestone, twenty-seven and half feet long. They even caught the attention of the professional journal of the stone industry, *Stone*, which published a photograph of the ledge in the quarry from which they were taken.[2] The purity of the stone could not be sufficiently praised: "a beautiful buff stone, absolutely free from flint, glass seams or imperfections of any kind." Chapin's instinct was correct— there is nothing like a single mighty block of stone, and with his portico he gave Williams its finest example of monumental sculpture.

After the grandiloquent Roman portico, the interior is a subtle essay in the interplay of light and dark. The entrance hall is a low space in dark wood, and its sense of enclosure and compression is given sudden release in the soaring lift of the interior. The sense of lift is enhanced by the transition from the lower level, which is paneled in dark quarter-sawn oak to the level of the gallery balustrade, to the upper level in ornamented and paneled white plaster. The theme of Gibbs's Senate House is carried out with marvelous fidelity: the same longitudinal plan, richly wainscoted ground story, balconies to either side, and wall articulation by means of the classical orders. There is even the same cross axis, with doors in the middle of the long sides for swiftly emptying the building. But Cram transformed his model into something more theatrical, placing a raised stage and proscenium at the far end, and sloping the floor to face it. The result is a hybrid of a debating hall and a theater, which was appropriate for the first building

from which Williams College students would graduate that was not religious in function but secular—and that worked very hard indeed to convey an equivalently ceremonial spectacle.

One should note the quiet intelligence of the details: the Ionic columns in unpainted wood over the stage that mirror their white-painted twins in the balcony above the entrance hall; the luxurious floor of alternating wide strips of teak and narrow ones of rosewood; and the organ cleverly inserted into the space above the stage, its sound filtering in through the grillwork about the proscenium lintel. One final note: Chapin Hall was originally named Grace Hall, in memory of Chapin's late wife. Sometime after his second marriage in 1913, the building was renamed Chapin Hall. Do we have the second Mrs. Chapin to thank for that?

61 Bernhard Music Center
Cambridge Seven Associates, 1979

To house the Music Department offices and classrooms next to their primary performance space in Chapin Hall, the college constructed a large addition alongside that building, clad in concrete, scored to resemble Renaissance rustication and to echo the stone quoins at the corners of Chapin. Here Walter Gropius's Masters Housing for the Bauhaus, Dessau, of the 1920s meets Renaissance Ferrara. Bernhard Music Center houses classrooms and offices at ground level and two auditoriums and a rehearsal room above. The latter spaces are reached by a broad staircase that leads to a well-lit hall and then the Presser Choral Hall and the Brooks Rogers Recital Hall. The scored concrete of the exterior continues into the reception area. Wood-paneled

H. Lee Hirsche with Georgia Glick, Rainspout Sculptures, 1979–80

Brooks Rogers is a successful multiuse space with excellent acoustics for recitals, but it is also set up with elaborate projection equipment so that the introductory art history course, which attracts big crowds, can take place there. At the upper level Bernhard is connected to Chapin, both to its public entrance hall and to the backstage area.

Visible from the upper reception hall, through plate glass walls, is the open space left between Chapin and Bernhard. This is an easy place to admire the cast stone sculpture that adorns Chapin. In the courtyard H. Lee Hirsche, who taught studio art for many years, in 1979–80 installed a highly imaginative series of metal sculptures that look like abstracted musical instruments. When it rains, water drips down into the sculptures, so they make sounds. In winter, drips of ice enliven the now silent, frozen forms.

62 Williams Hall
Cram, Goodhue & Ferguson, 1910–12

Sage Hall
Cram & Ferguson, 1922

Without a question, the loveliest passage of the entire Williams College campus is the Freshman Quadrangle, the landscape yard enclosed by Chapin, Williams, and Sage Halls. It fulfills the vision of the Olmsted brothers, who in 1902 proposed that the college group all its new buildings according to function in quadrangles, the classrooms and administration along Main Street and the dormitories moved to the periphery. When Alfred Chapin donated a new auditorium in 1909, President Garfield saw an opportunity to make it the centerpiece of one of the college's first comprehensively designed quadrangles, and this was the challenge presented to the architect, Ralph Adams Cram.

Cram's design was beautifully modulated to put Chapin Hall at the head of a monumental axis, giving it pride of place; the dormitories took up a deferential position to the side, standing far enough back to allow diagonal views toward the distant mountains. Despite the formal symmetry, there is nothing stiff about the quad. The axis that runs between the Symmes Memorial Gate and Chapin Hall is not a ceremonial path at all, since it leads to a door that is almost never opened. Rather, it is a purely visual axis, giving a pleasing sense of order that helps us calibrate our sense of freedom.

Williams and Sage, as Cram explained, "adhere more closely to the English Georgian type than to its derivative, American Colonial." He recognized that nothing so grand ever existed in eighteenth-century America, where there was neither the financial wherewithal nor the trained craftsmen nor the architectural knowledge. Nonetheless, if those provincial builders could make only crude

ABOVE **Williams Hall** RIGHT **Sage Hall**

approximations of the work of Christopher Wren or James Gibbs, the aspiration was there. Cram's buildings propose what their buildings might have looked like had they had the means and knowledge. For one thing, they would have been amply and richly ornamented. Williams and Sage brim with carved detail in Indiana limestone: belt courses, keystones, window surrounds, pediments, the carved shields at the end blocks, and the rather burly bracketed cornice. Even the brick is used for sculptural effect, the various entries stepping forward and back, and forming hefty quoins at the corners. The round windows are especially handsome, their carved details pinched from Wren's palace at Hampton Court. Naturally, all this was an architectural expression of Anglophilia and to a worshipful extent. Cram himself spoke approvingly of such architecture as *ethnic poetry*.

Williams Hall was the first to be built, but unlike Chapin, it was not fully funded. Despite substantial gifts from the Classes of 1882 and 1885, there was only enough for the Park Street wing; in the end, Francis Stetson—perhaps wishing to help Chapin, his fraternity brother—intervened with a $60,000 gift. The crossarm was added one year later and completed in 1912. Because there was no principal donor, the building was called Williams Hall; its rental income, as was typical in those days, was applied to a specific need—an overdue increase in the salary of Williams professors from $3,000 to $4,000 (and for assistant professors, from $2,000 to $3,000).

Because of the slowness in fundraising and the disruptions of World War I, Sage Hall was not built until 1923. It is an exact mirror image of Williams Hall—or so everyone believes. But the entablature is simpler (it omits the egg-and-dart molding), and if one counts the windows along Park Street, one sees that Sage has significantly more dormitory rooms. This is architectural achievement of a high order, to squeeze a dozen more students into a building that is for all practical purposes identical.

63   Symmes Memorial Gate
Cram & Ferguson, 1936

Cram's intention from the very beginning was that Williams and Sage Halls be connected by a monumental gate. (See p. 36.) This was not built until 1936 and only then because of a tragedy. Professor Herdman F. Cleland and three students sailing to the Yucatan to study Mayan ruins died when the passenger liner *Mohawk* collided with a freighter and sank. The Symmes Memorial Gate was given as a memorial by the father of one of the students. Their names are recorded on the gate, along with a poignant verse by Robert Louis Stevenson. The scheme of brick and limestone piers, joined by hefty wrought-iron work, is much as Cram designed it a quarter century earlier, but with one melancholy addition—the funereal urns that top the piers.

64   Lehman Hall
Cram & Ferguson, 1927

Prior to the conversion of Lawrence Hall to the college art museum in 1926, it was used in part as a freshman dormitory. Having dislodged these students and needing to house them, the college asked Cram & Ferguson to design a new dormitory, in "colonial architecture to match the other dormitories." Several sites were considered. The best was on Park Street, where the student center now stands, to continue the line of Williams and Sage. But this implied a building of equal quality—and cost. And so when Cram submitted three designs that November, he offered a range of choices, from an ambitious $105,000 dormitory for thirty-two students to a simpler $47,000 dormitory for thirty students. President Garfield chose the inexpensive design.

Inexpensive, but not inelegant. Lehman is a handsomely detailed and proportioned composition, with two graceful but simple entrance porticos of wood (much of Cram's savings came from substituting wood for stone ornament). Also handsome is the detailing of the interior, with trim in birch and pine, and bathrooms of white marble. The building would look less forlorn had Cram's plans been realized. He envisioned a second identical dormitory just to the east, to form a matching pair much like Williams and Sage. Yet it was the great misfortune of Lehman to have been completed just before the Great Depression, which put an abrupt stop to the college's building program. But the site was kept open, and much later in 1972, the plan was revived by a local architect, William Kirby, who submitted a more utilitarian floor plan (presumably without the pine, birch, and marble trim). Although drawings were made, this too was postponed. The site remained vacant until 2008, when it was claimed by Hollander Hall, thereby ensuring that Lehman would forever remain twinless.

The donor was Herbert H. Lehman, a member of the Class of 1899 and one of the first significant Jewish graduates of Williams College. A partner at Lehman Brothers, he was elected governor of New York four times and twice senator.

65   Mears House (Theta Delta Chi)
Cram & Ferguson, 1925

For much of their history, the fraternity houses of Williams College were more sophisticated architecturally than its dormitories. This changed with Williams and Sage, buildings as elegant and fashionable as anything in Williamstown. Now fraternities no longer asserted distinctive individual identity but sought instead to look like the natural extension of the college. Theta Delta Chi took the process to its logical conclusion, not only building a fraternity house that looked like Williams and Sage, but even hiring the same architects.

Mears House, its current name, is a studied performance in the Georgian Revival, based loosely on Carter's Grove (1750), perhaps the finest of eighteenth-century Virginia houses. Only the projecting vestibule, a miniature temple in its own right, warns of the Massachusetts winter. The facade is a seven-bay, symmetrical composition, saved from stiffness by the projecting one-and-a-half-story dependency to the north. (The dining room was originally located here.) The brickwork, laid in Flemish bond, is of the highest quality. A clever touch is the brick belt course, which serves only to cap the segmental arches of the first-story windows and then stops. The hefty end chimneys, the crisply drawn cornice, the alternation of segmental

and triangular dormers—everything is finely considered and detailed. The interior with its splendid woodwork is worth a visit. (The building now serves Alumni Relations.) Unfortunately, the secondary entrance and private stair, through which returning members once could slip upstairs discreetly, is no longer usable, although it is outwardly expressed in the attractively detailed projecting bay on the south wall.

Mears House's most unusual feature, its generous front yard, is the by-product of a building decision. It was built behind the fraternity's original wooden home, which was demolished only when the new building was finished. The pragmatic brothers of Theta Delta Chi did not want to be homeless for even a minute.

66　St. John's Episcopal Church

Rotch & Tilden,
1894–96

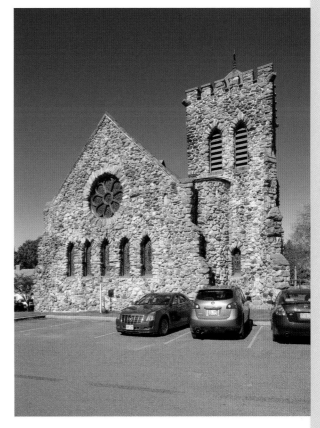

Congregationalist Williams College was not necessarily welcoming to other Protestant religions seeking to gain a foothold in the town. The first Episcopal service in Williamstown was conducted in 1853 in a private home by a freshman, William Tatlock, who had been born in England. At that time, a faculty member who served as a preacher in the Meeting House allowed that he found "little difference between Episcopals and Catholics."

Rich summer residents, who brought their own religion with them, were the force behind establishing a parish in 1894 and ultimately building St. John's, consecrated in 1896. Donors included Harley Proctor, of Proctor and Gamble, and Mrs. Eugene Jerome, whose daughter Jenny was the mother of Winston Churchill. This cannot have been agreeable to the college. In the same year that it had acquired and razed St. Patrick's on the corner of Main and Park Streets, it had to face the opening, just a few steps down Park Street, of a building whose worshippers were "little" different from "papists."

Ralph Adams Cram supplied a design for the new St. John's, but it was not built. Instead, a building with superb stonework by Norcross, the construction firm that worked for the great Henry Hobson Richardson, rose on the site where once a Congregational lecture hall had stood. Proctor donated the glacial fieldstones from property he owned on Stone Hill, which rises behind the Clark Art Institute. In bright sun, the sheer stoniness of the stone walls is spectacular.

67 Faculty House
Thomas Harlan Ellett, 1938–39; Cambridge Seven Associates, 1983

In 1938 Clark Williams, a member of the Class of 1892, gave $100,000 for a "palatial" Williams College faculty house that would provide for the "social, scholastic and education use and activities of the members of the faculty and the administrative staff of the college and their wives."[3] It is significant that he mentioned *wives*. Until this moment the buildings at the all-male college had deliberately cultivated a kind of hearty, manly character. This may account for the donor's choice of architect, Thomas Harlan Ellett, who had just designed the Cosmopolitan Club in New York, one of America's most fashionable women's clubs.

In February 1938 Ellett published a design for a two-story Georgian Revival building with a pedimented portico. It was a handsome building that looked a bit too much like a private house, which may explain why he produced a second design in July of entirely different character, more a templelike pavilion. The introverted house now became an extroverted club, welcoming visitors with broad Tuscan porticos on both Main and Park Streets. At this point, however, hardly anybody believed in pedimented porticos anymore. A perceptive 1939 editorial in the *North Adams Transcript* complained that the building's "heavy outline accentuated by its square and squatty brick pillars contrasts so strangely with the exquisite old-time charm, so completely appropriate to its setting, of the President's House of the opposite corner." (The *Williams Record* made the same point in 1952, although in more forceful student language, when it called it "a glorified gas station.")

The interior is worth a visit, especially to see the unpainted ceiling of "pecky cypress," a stressed wood surface caused by pocket rot (the action of the fungus *Stereum taxodii*). And note also the pine cones at the cornice corners. The portrait over the fireplace of the donor with the Williams family dog (a symbol of faculty gratitude?) was by Edwin Megargee, a specialist in painting hunting dogs. (One should also inspect the nearby portrait of Williams's wife by the fashionable Swiss painter Adolfo Müller-Ury.) One

should forgive the donor these tiny bits of personal vanity—after all, Mr. Williams could hardly name the building after himself.

Philanthropy was certainly in Clark Williams's blood. His aunt was Mrs. Frederick F. Thompson, who gave the Thompson Memorial Chapel, and he himself had founded the Williams Club in New York in 1913. He directed the field services of the American Red Cross during the closing army offensives of World War I. Besides paying for the faculty house, he also contributed heavily to the 1936 squash courts.

In 1983 the job of enlarging the Faculty House was given to Cambridge Seven Associates, whose Bernhard addition to Chapin Hall showed that they knew how to add a modern wing to a historic building, sensitively and imaginatively. Here they fashioned a modern abstraction of the original building, a particularly happy addition that somehow manages to improve the original building and relieve what had been rather cramped and stuffy spaces.

68   '62 Center for Theatre and Dance
William Rawn Associates, 2005

Dominating the north side of Main Street between the Faculty House and the Greylock Quadrangle is the out-of-scale mass of the '62 Center for Theatre and Dance, an expression of the triumph of architectural ego over the character of the architecture. The building has its enthusiasts, among whom are not the authors and photographer of these pages.

The dramatically projecting, tall-but-narrow entrance lobby, its thin glass walls capped with a roof that flares up and out, dominates everything around it. Behind that wall is a curving stone wall that echoes the shape of the auditorium inside. There are multiple sources for these forms, not all apt for a theater design.

In the nineteenth century the German architect Gottfried Semper designed a theater on the central square of Dresden, opposite the ruler's palace. Jutting out from the curved exterior of the auditorium is a rectangular solid facing the palace. From this projection the Elector of Saxony could show himself to his subjects from a royal balcony. Thus a political purpose stood behind this unusual theater design. Rawn's uncomfortably tall and narrow entrance hall seems a poor substitute. The flared roof is lifted from Louis I. Kahn's unbuilt design of around 1970 for the Hurva Synagogue in Jerusalem. For the hardly religious Kahn, synagogues were educational institutions, symbolized by a teacher under a tree. Almost all of Kahn's synagogue designs have references to trees. In Jerusalem, four enormous, abstract concrete trees with flaring planes for branches would have held up the synagogue roof. Kahn's form had both profound meaning and dramatic visual presence. Here the form is just an attention-getter, with no meaning beyond that. The curved wall behind the entrance hall features a diagonal projection that wraps around it like one of the curves on the outside of Frank Lloyd Wright's Guggenheim Museum, opened in 1959, in New York. When the building was still in the design stage, one of us asked an administrator of the college if this projection indicated the presence of a ramp or staircase. The administrator drew a blank. The curve is gratuitous decoration.

Inside, the auditorium, at the behest of the main donor, has the U-shape of an Italian opera house, a type of theater with notoriously bad sight lines, in which it is as important to see the people in the boxes, and for them to see you, as it is to view the action on stage. There are no boxes here, however. The acoustics are poor, and the light-wood interior, insisted on by the architect, prevents a director from achieving a totally dark space to set off a single spot on stage. The dance studio to the rear, however, is said to be a delight to work in, and it enjoys great views of the mountains.

Attached to the west of the Rawn building is the stub of what was once the Adams Memorial Theater, a Cram design of 1941. Cram was assisted by Stanley McCandles of the Yale Drama School in designing a theater that was state of the art in its day. Cram's original design (by someone in his office), accepted by the trustees, was not a nostalgic Georgian confection but something that belonged to the governmental, sandblasted classicism style of its day. In the end, Georgian won out, and the theater came to have a Tuscan portico of white columns supporting a white pediment, all poised against a red brick exterior. (See p. 44.)

Rawn tore off the face of the building, claiming that his new design went back to Cram's original idea and comported better with his own Semper-Kahn-Wright confection. In so doing, he eliminated one of the several classical porticos that had come consistently to characterize that stretch of Main Street. If an architect of the genius of Francesco Borromini could leave the mediocre

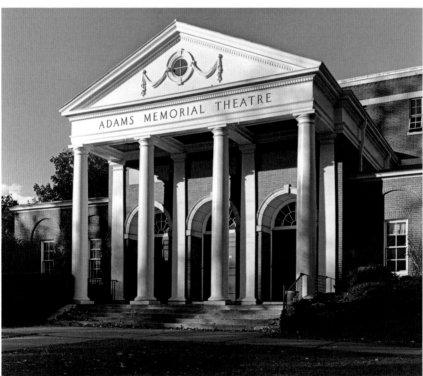

Cram & Ferguson, Adams Memorial Theater, 1941. The building is incorporated into the '62 Center for Theatre and Dance, minus its handsome portico.

'62 Center for Theatre and Dance, MainStage auditorium

'62 Center for Theatre and Dance, Dance Studio

facade of the sixteenth-century Chiesa Nuova in Rome alone when he built his own brilliant facade of the Oratorio di San Filippo Neri, begun in 1637, next to it, then such architectural vandalism as Rawn's is not necessary to create a great building. If you really want to see the worst of this building, take a look at the visual chaos of the thoughtless way Rawn left the west side of the old Adams Memorial Theater, facing the Greylock Quadrangle.

69 Parking Garage
William Rawn Associates, 2003

How often does one read a glowing review of a parking garage? Usually they offend the eye. This garage, however, calls for admiration for its sensitivity to its site, not only in terms of its curved shape but also in terms of its use of materials that are compatible with the nearby Greylock Quadrangle. The three-story structure is tucked into the ground so that it reads mostly as a two-story building with a floating tiara. The whole is a long, leisurely, sweeping arc that follows the contours of the slope into which it is set. The horizontal parapet walls that alternate with ventilating voids are faced with brick that matches that of Greylock, capped by a concrete layer tinted to accord with the brick. Atop the third story is an airfoil-shaped "roof" that serves no particular function save to echo the gray concrete cornices of Greylock and the curvature of the plan of the garage, which makes a fitting foil for the angular geometry of the dormitories. On the north side of the structure, curving brick walls hide huge pieces of mechanical equipment that serve the '62 Center for Theatre and Dance, just as the garage itself serves the patrons of that building, particularly the crowds that flock in summertime to the presentations of the Williamstown Theater Festival. Would that all parking garages enhanced their surroundings so handsomely.

Across North Street from the open field between the garage and Greylock Quadrangle is the Williamstown Town Hall, formerly the Phi Gamma Delta Fraternity House (1928), one of the architecturally least distinguished of the frat lodges. The architect was Alfred Busselle, a Quaker architect from New York who specialized in tasteful country houses. His Phi Gamma Delta, he claimed, was "an innovation in Williamstown as it is a style borrowed for the first time from further South." How far south he did not say. The fraternity sold the house to the town in 1965, much to the annoyance of the college. Student visits to the building, which houses the police station at the rear, are not always as pleasant as they were when it was still a fraternity, and the resident cook played jazz trumpet.

70 George Warren Rickey, *Double L Excentric Gyratory II*, 1981, stainless steel

Williams College Museum of Art, inaugural gift of the Class of 1961 Public Art Fund on the occasion of their fiftieth reunion

Traditional sculpture does not move. Inspired by the early twentieth-century movement of constructivism, George Rickey's sculpture does. Motionless when the air is still, or gyrating slowly in a storm, Rickey's twin Ls simultaneously make us aware of the unpredictable power of nature and the controlled clarity of geometry. Elegantly engineered to take anything the weather can hand out, this work rotates on its slender pole to accompany the curving path below it— the result of a knowing choice by the donors and the college administration of a site on the campus for a sculpture whose creator designed it with no particular site in mind. The glistening, machine-brushed surface of the contemporary material, shiny steel, flickers as the parts move.

71   Greylock Quadrangle
Benjamin Thompson, The Architects Collaborative, 1963–65

Two major projects to provide housing and dining for students resulted from the decision by Jack Sawyer to replace the functions of fraternities at Williams: Greylock Quadrangle and Mission Park Housing. Greylock is sited on the very lot reserved in the 1750 plan for the minister. The minister quickly sold the lot, which became the location of the town tavern and, later, the Greylock Hotel. Housing transients has, in a sense, been the constant role of this property. In the case of the dormitories, the student occupants were invited to participate in the design process, to the point of living in and assessing mock-ups of dorm rooms set up inside the college gymnasium.

In October 1963 the trustees viewed plans and models of four dormitory buildings, or residential houses, and one dining hall building to feed the inhabitants of all the dorms, to be erected on the Greylock site. Under the Baxter regime, during the meeting of the trustees at which Sawyer was elected president, a design by Shepley Bulfinch Richardson and Abbott had been approved for that very same site, but after the inauguration of Sawyer, that design disappears from the Trustees' Minutes. It surely did not conform to Sawyer's vision of small residential houses.[4] Nor, one suspects, did it suit his modernist sensibilities. A Ford Foundation challenge grant of $2.5 million, to match by three times the amount raised by the college, arrived just in time to help underwrite the cost of the project, which was estimated at $3.37 million, without furnishings.[5]

The major problem Benjamin Thompson, principal designer, faced was the steep eastward slope of the land down toward the theater. The boxy dormitories step down the slope, their structure of brick-bearing walls supporting reinforced concrete lintels on the exterior and reinforced concrete floor slabs with a waffle pattern on the ceilings inside. He arranged L-shaped towers in an irregular pattern that did not create an actual quadrangle but the feeling of an irregular, relaxed enclosure without closing off views to the surrounding countryside. The dark windows visually break up the masses of the exteriors, and some provide views of the surrounding mountains. Skillful plantings of mature evergreens integrated the dorms with nature from the beginning. This may be the most satisfying outdoor space ever built on the campus; it encloses but never entraps.

A separate two-story building for dining and classrooms forms the eastern edge of the complex, intervening between dorms and the tower of the fly space of the Adams Memorial Theater. Thompson's Greylock Dining Hall actually made that tower seem to belong to the whole site, whereas before it had conjured up an alien presence in the campus. Three dining rooms, one large and two small, are reached by a handsome staircase that opens up to tall

Greylock Quadrangle;
in foreground, Isaac Witkin, Succoth, 1975

Greylock Dining Hall

ceilings and expansive glass walls. The large hall was designed to accommodate dances. Cutting expenses after the Great Recession of 2008, the college closed the dining hall, but the classrooms at ground level are still open.

Thompson, formerly a pupil of Walter Gropius at Harvard, had become the latter's colleague in The Architects Collaborative. Aerial views of Greylock reveal how Thompson had picked up Gropius's technique of designing flat-roofed, asymmetrical buildings, exemplified by the famous Bauhaus (1926) in Dessau, Germany. Gropius was quite keen on how buildings looked from the new vantage point of the airplane. Williams gave Gropius an honorary degree in 1963, a recognition not only of his importance in the history of twentieth-century architecture but also of the move of Williams into the twentieth century architecturally under the leadership of Sawyer.

72   Field Park

Regulation House, 1953, with later repairs

Field Park, the attractively landscaped park at the junction of Routes 7 and 2, is a vestige of Williamstown's original town green, transformed into something that its original creators could never have envisioned. In the seventeenth and eighteenth centuries, a town greens was a useful place, the focus of community life but also an area where animals could graze. As town greens grew in sentimental and historical interest, their meaning changed, and in the nineteenth century they came to be seen as aesthetic objects. An opportunity arose in Williamstown, when the Congregational Meeting House left its traditional place at the head of the town green to be closer to the college. This move left its original site neglected and bereft, something that was put right by the creation of Field Park, one of the great, selfless acts of philanthropy in the history of Williamstown.

Cyrus W. Field, the visionary who created the transatlantic cable, did not graduate from Williams College, but several of his brothers did. He too became a loyal benefactor, and in 1877 he gave $10,000 to beautify Williamstown, which

Kappa Alpha, Williams College's first Victorian fraternity building. According to a contemporary description, it "fronts Field Park. The studies, bedrooms and library are below, assembly and lodge-rooms above. The first story is built of brick, with granite foundation and trimmings; the second story and cupola, of wood; cost, about $15,000." (*Delta Upsilon Quarterly*, May 1885)

Kappa Alpha Lodge, Williams College

Harley T. Procter was the advertising genius who won fame as "the Ivory soap king." According to the amusing (but untrue) campus legend, he abandoned Williamstown because students constantly shouted at him—mocking his soap advertisement—"does it really float?" His house was designed by the Lowell firm of Stickney & Austin.

then engaged B. S. Olmsted, a very capable landscape architect of Rye, New York (not to be confused with F. L. Olmsted of Central Park, although their principles were much the same). Olmsted proposed to bring the entire town

> into a single scheme of decorative treatment, terracing and planting and turfing, and adapting the whole embellishment to the suggestions which the lay of the land naturally furnishes, as well as to the convenience of the inhabitants; taking away fences and hedges, damming up a convenient stream to form a lake and waterfall, and converting the whole into a continuous park.[6]

The proposal to turn an entire town into "a continuous park" was wildly radical for the time; the influential *American Architect* praised the scheme as "perhaps the first instance in the country where a town already existing has been taken up with the purpose of making the most of its natural characteristics, and applying a decorative landscape treatment to the whole town." Within a few years, Field Park was a picturesquely landscaped park with meandering paths, open meadow, and clumps of trees.

Almost simultaneous with the new picturesque treatment of the landscape came the first studiously picturesque fraternity house, Kappa Alpha, which was built in 1877 near the site of the first Meeting House. The architects were William

TOP **Reconstruction of Regulation House, 1958**
BOTTOM **Reconstruction of Regulation House, interior**

A. Potter (himself a Kappa Alpha from Union College) and Robert H. Robertson, and together they built a willfully spiky essay in timber, brick, and granite. Placed at the town's most conspicuous intersection, the building drew considerable attention, and other fraternity houses soon built their own flamboyant ripostes.

It is amusing to learn that the members of this swaggering fraternity eventually moved into one of Williamstown's most tasteful buildings—just to the left in the photograph. (See p. 219.) This was the house of Harley T. Procter, the imperious Procter & Gamble heir. He built the palatial mansion in the late 1890s but spent only a few summers there. Annoyed at the poor condition of the Williamstown roads, which spoiled his daily carriage ride, he offered to pay $10,000 (was he echoing Field's gift?) to have them paved. There was one condition: he was to decide where and how the money was to be spent, a condition that the town could not accept. In a fit of pique, he abandoned his house, which was taken over by Kappa Alpha in 1905. (Bizarrely, he passed on the feud to his children: when Lilian, his daughter, sold her New Ashford estate in 1950, she stipulated that it not be sold to anyone from Williamstown, whatever the price.) The house burned in 1966, just after the fraternity sold it to the college. It is now the site of the Williams Inn.

In 1953, to celebrate the bicentennial of Williamstown, Field Park was once again given a comprehensive restoration—but this time it drew its inspiration not from Central Park but from the fastidious re-creation of Colonial Williamsburg. A group of local volunteers, directed by Henry N. Flynt Jr., an alumnus (Class of 1944) and director of Student Aid whose family had restored Historic Deerfield, Massachusetts, joined forces to build a replica of the first houses raised in Williamstown in the 1750s. They used the same tools and the same locally available materials, and they availed themselves of information provided by still-preserved elements of original houses. The result is an extremely careful reconstruction of the typical "Regulation House" that each purchaser of a lot in West Hoosac was required to construct. The early settlers of the town brought with them traditions of wood architecture that they had known in Connecticut or around Deerfield. Two men, helping each other, could probably raise two houses in three months, in time to install their families in the fall, before the snow flew. Each house was required to be at least fifteen feet by eighteen feet, with a ceiling height of seven feet. A single fireplace, with a chimney made of local fieldstone, kept the settlers warm against the frigid winter. A loft provided extra sleeping space, as the number of children in the family grew. These houses could be easily enlarged by adding on a replica of the first to create a house with a footprint of thirty feet by fifteen feet, with a second chimney, back to back with the first, to heat the new space.

ENDNOTES

1 Charles C. Grant, "Rebuilding of the First Congregational Church, Williamstown, Mass.,"
   Architecture, 1915, 251.

2 "The New Giberson Quarry at Bedford," *Stone* 32, no. 7 (July 1911): 371–82.

3 "$100,000 Faculty House Presented to Williams," *North Adams Transcript,* February 14,
   1938, 3.

4 Williams College Trustees' Minutes, January 21, 1961.

5 Williams College Trustees' Minutes, October 4, 1963, note Ford Foundation Grant
   received.

6 *American Architect and Building News* 2, no. 77 (June 16, 1877): 186.

The former fraternity houses that line the south side of Main Street form a particularly strong element in the townscape. All resemble large residences of the rich from the period in which they were built, which is no accident: the buildings housed, in the days before World War II and even after, the sons of the rich in a style that included resident cooks and servants. In all, there were fifteen fraternities at Williams; the houses of two commanded the north and south sides of Field Park, and the rest were scattered around town. The seven at the west end of Main Street greeted the visitor to Williamstown entering from the south, on US Route 7, and created the impression of having arrived at a special place in a rural landscape. Six still stand.

Fraternities arrived at Williams in the 1830s, but they did not make a strong architectural impact on the town until several decades later, when individual chapters began to build ever more extravagant living and meeting quarters. The Stick Style Kappa Alpha House (1877) was an outstanding example of their architectural braggadocio. (See p. 219.) Wooden buildings, however, fell out of fashion, both because of changing styles and because they were too susceptible to disastrous fires. Toward the end of the century, masonry Colonial Revival houses became the standard, before the same style became the *lingua classica* of the college. By roughly 1910 most of Williams's frat houses had been built. Fraternities almost always seemed to have more money at their disposal than the college, and their architecture tended to be both more lavish and more up-to-date. Frat brothers inhabited the kinds of architecture to which their parents had accustomed them.

By the 1960s student life and fraternity life at Williams were virtually synonymous: 44 percent of the students lived in fraternities, and practically all of them (94 percent of upperclassmen) took their meals there. But during these same years, with the triumph of the civil rights movement, the socially exclusive policies of some fraternities were drawing unwelcome attention. In 1962 the trustees at last took a critical look at the fraternity question and issued what became known as the *Angevine Report*, which recommended the complete abolition of fraternities.

> Long continued delegation to the fraternities by the College of a large part of its responsibility with respect to the housing, feeding, and social accommodations of the student body is a major cause of many existing conditions which are harmful to the educational purpose of the College; and early steps should be taken by the College to re-assume this responsibility and integrate these functions into the life of the College, where they properly belong.

It took three years for the fraternities to dissolve themselves and to convey most of their properties to Williams. By 1965 all of them had, with the exception of Phi Gamma Delta, which in a fit of pique sold its building to the town of Williamstown to serve as the new town hall. All but one of the other former fraternity houses, the demolished Sigma Phi, are now used by the college as dormitories or offices. The largest concentration consists of the five Main Street houses that constitute Fraternity Row. They are presented below, from east to west.

73 Spencer House (Chi Psi)
James Purdon, 1908–9

Fraternities often took their cues from their neighboring institutions, and Chi Psi was an especially avid borrower. In the early 1880s Robert S. Stephenson designed Chi Psi houses for both Amherst (his alma mater) and Williams College. A generation later, Chi Psi moved out, sold its building to Williams, which used it as its first Faculty Club, and proceeded to build a new and larger chapter house. Once again it copied. This time the model was the Delphic Club (1903) at Harvard, and its architect, James Purdon, was summoned to Williamstown to deliver as close a paraphrase as possible. Purdon felt perfectly free to plagiarize from himself: Spencer House (its current name) has the same scheme of projecting pedimented blocks flanking a recessed central entrance, the same brick and limestone details, even the same Doric portico with paired columns as his Harvard design.

Purdon, an 1895
Harvard graduate,
had more to offer than
several toney clubhouses
at Harvard. He was a
specialist in the innovative
use of concrete, which
was attractive to a
campus that had recently
lost several fraternity
houses to fire. Purdon,
accordingly, made
Spencer as fireproof
as possible, building its
walls of concrete block
and its floors of "poured
concrete, reinforced with

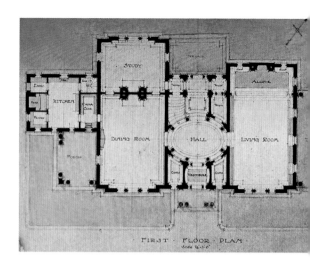

Spencer House has Williams College's most stylish entrance hall, a graceful ellipse offering a range of possible paths of movement.

steel."[1] (The same system of construction, he noted, had just been used in the college's Berkshire Hall.) There was an added benefit in that each of the twelve bedrooms upstairs was completely soundproof.

At first glance, the interior looks like a straightforward center hall plan, but Purdon's written description reveals how thoughtfully he considered the placement and treatment of each space:

> The front door opens into a vestibule leading to the hall. The latter is designed in the shape of an ellipse, so as to allow space for a lavatory and coat and telephone rooms. A passage leads from this hall straight out onto the terrace at the rear. At the left will be the spacious dining-room, which is to open at the west end into a library. The latter room is so arranged that it can be easily converted into an auxiliary dining-room. The kitchen and its accessories are located on this floor in a shoulder at the south end. The smoking-room occupies the north end of the house and opens out onto the Main Street veranda mentioned above. Library, dining-room and study contain large fireplaces, and the wainscoting, paneled ceilings and other trimmings are to be of chestnut.[2]

Purdon was the only architect to build a fraternity at Williams who recognized the problem of the Fraternity Row site. Slung out along the south side of Main Street, the fraternities inevitably faced north, condemning all the principal rooms to perpetually gloomy northern light. Purdon swiveled his building to run north–south, which gave every room eastern or western exposure, meaning they would get ample light at some point in the day. This put the principal facade on Hoxsey Street, facing the college. But Main Street could not be snubbed, and there, if only for the sake of decorum, he placed a colonnaded portico. Over the years, many must have been surprised when they tried to enter, only to discover that they had arrived at the fraternity's smoking porch.

74 Brooks House (Delta Kappa Epsilon)

Daniel O'Connell & Sons, 1961

TOP **Delta Kappa Epsilon's original fraternity house was designed by Lamb & Rich, a busy New York firm that regularly worked in Williamstown. At the time it was built (1897), the college had not yet decided if its new buildings would be in Colonial Revival or Gothic. Grand and stylish fraternity houses like this helped tip the scale in favor of the former.**

In the winter of 1959 a dramatic fire, apparently set by a fraternity member to destroy the records of his embezzlements from his brothers, razed the old Deke House, an 1897 example of *Gone with the Wind* gone "Nawth," designed by Lamb & Rich. In what was doubtless an attempt to restore its damaged public image, the fraternity decided to "break with the prevailing style of fraternity houses on the Williams campus, nearly all of which are in traditional modes."[3] Philip S. Collins (Class of 1950), who recently passed through Princeton's school

RIGHT AND BOTTOM **Jules Gregory's 1959 design for what is now Brooks House would have given Williams its first modern fraternity building. But somewhere along the way, the design lost the best aspect of modernism, which is the graceful expression of construction, and retained its worst—a ruthless indifference to context.**

of architecture, recommended Jules Gregory, a young architect who had just won fame with his innovative Butterfly House. Gregory produced a fiercely contemporary design that consisted of little more than tapered reinforced-concrete columns and a continuous wall of glass. The modernist faction of the Williams Art Department, led by Whitney Stoddard, supported the daring design, a model of which was exhibited in Lawrence Hall.

In the end, Gregory's design was not built. Builders' estimates came in $100,000 above what the fraternity had to spend, and by the time it reassessed its options, the radical fervor had subsided. The project was put in the hands of a highly practical firm of Massachusetts builder-architects, who pushed it in a more traditional direction. The cubic massing and low hipped roof were retained, but Gregory's structural columns were pushed forward to become a crudely abstract version of the classical portico of the original 1897 house. The result, neither modern nor historicizing, is the worst of both worlds. It is a sad comment on the fate of classical architecture in the post-World War II era.

75   Weston Hall (Phi Delta Theta)
Squires & Wynkoop, 1905–7; Rear addition:
Architectural Resources Cambridge, 2015

First converted from fraternity use as the Weston Language Center, where all foreign languages were taught, this glowering cliff of a house with its vaguely Dutch detail is a thoughtful response to its setting, both natural and historical: "The steep pitched roof is fitting to the northern mountainous region and the twin-columned portico, without taking emphasis in the design, suggests the architectural traditions of a district settled at an early date."[4] So wrote the architect, Frederick A. Squires (Class of 1900), who was both a member of Phi Delta Theta and one of three brothers who attended Williams.

Squires's design was innovative enough to be published in the key professional journals. The *Architectural Record* published its unusual floor plan, while the *International Studio* noted its ingenious use of brick: "Care has been taken to effect a pleasant variety of surface in the brick walls by recessed courses, trims, inlays, marked-out window spaces and occasional patterns."[5] One of those occasional patterns has been the subject of recent controversy. A reviewer noted that "the club's symbols have been executed in colored tile and inserted into the brickwork. The Swastika, emblem of mystery, shows between the first story windows surrounded by a brick pattern which is evidently symbolic."[6] A swastika, of course, had a different meaning in 1909. The ancient symbol was not tainted with Nazism, which did not yet exist, and was merely a decorative motif (one whose orientation the Nazis reversed in order to claim it as their own). Nonetheless, when the building was converted to the

admissions office, the college administration decided it did not want to have to explain repeatedly to prospective students the form's historical origins, and it insisted that every swastika be masked by a blank panel.

In fact, the brothers of Phi Delta Theta were no Nazis. In 1953 the Williams College chapter was suspended from the national fraternity "for pledging a Jewish student in violation of a clause in the national constitution that restricts membership to 'men of white and full Aryan blood.'"[7] All fifty-seven Williams members voted unanimously to admit the student, and the incident caused a national scandal, sending a shock wave through the entire ΦΔΘ fraternity organization. Within two years its discrimination policy was revoked—a reform set in motion, ironically, from inside the building with the swastikas.

Since 2015 Weston has housed the Offices of Admissions and Student Aid, for which Architectural Resources Cambridge provided a symmetrically planned, two-story, more-or-less-modern addition to the rear. The orange-brown masonry of the exterior of the block-like extension is sympathetic to the colors of the original building. It is a tail that happily does not try to wag the old dog to which it is attached.

76 Jewish Religious Center
Herbert Newman Associates, 1990

Tucked away on Stetson Court, the Jewish Religious Center is the first building the college ever erected for a religion that was not the Protestant faith of its founders. Up until the late twentieth century, Williams, like many other private institutions in the United States, was not particularly hospitable to Jews. There were a few Jewish students, often from wealthy New York families, and also a few scholarship students. Because there was no synagogue in town, a small space was made available in the basement of Thompson Memorial Chapel for Jewish use. In the days when attendance at a religious service was required of all students, at least biweekly, nominally Christian students would go to Jewish services on Fridays to keep their weekends free. That all

changed during the Oakley administration, when the Jewish presence on campus was celebrated by the construction of this building. (Compulsory attendance at religious services had been eliminated under the Sawyer regime.) Given the now greatly increased number of students at Williams who belong to other world faiths, it is appropriate for the college to afford them equal status on campus by constructing visible and suitable structures for their use.

The severely planar, symmetrical exterior, marked by eight chimneys at its corners, is dominated by an octagon that rises from a centrally placed square and terminates in a four-sided, truncated pyramid. (A Jewish faculty member wryly commented on a "superfluity of chimneys.") Below this vertical accent is the central meeting space, a polygon crowned by a skylight with a six-pointed star. The eastern walls of the polygon can be raised to expand the interior when more space is required.

77   Bascom House (Beta Theta Pi)
Harding & Seaver, 1913

78   Horn Hall Dormitory
Centerline Architects, 2016

79   Perry House (Alpha Delta Phi)
Russell Sturgis, 1868; Jerome Ripley Allen, 1905

When in need of an architect, fraternities always turned to a brother first. Alpha Delta Phi did it twice. In 1868 it hired Russell Sturgis, then the only practicing architect in the United States who was an Alpha Delta Phi member. His building was an odd, belligerently angular Gothic pavilion, a miniature version of the neo-Gothic dormitories he was then building at Yale. When that style became unpopular, Alpha Delta Phi summoned Jerome Ripley Allen, who had gone to Columbia's School of Architecture after graduating from Williams in 1895. He transformed Sturgis's chapter house into the building now known as Perry House, a refined and urbane essay in the Colonial Revival.

The original chapter house of Alpha Delta Phi was never demolished; its walls were incorporated into what is now Perry House.

Allen's building set in motion a wave of frenetic building activity on Fraternity Row, which alarmed President Harry Hopkins. The new chapter houses were much larger than their Victorian precursors, and he feared that a significant proportion of the student body could spend their college career living there, isolated from campus life. But his criticism was muted. After all, he himself was an Alpha Delta Phi brother. And so were two of his wealthiest and most generous alumni, Francis Stetson (Class of 1867) and Alfred Chapin (Class of 1869). There was no move to stop the building wave, and within four years Wood House, Weston House, and Spencer House were built, each of them in proudly Colonial Revival style.

Perry House was repeatedly enlarged and remodeled, in 1914, 1929, and again in 1970. Of the college's former fraternity houses, it contains the best-preserved "goat room," fraternity slang for the meeting room.

80 Wood House (Zeta Psi)
William Neil Smith, 1907; Addition, 1927

Built within a few years of one another, the buildings of Fraternity Row are of the same basic type but with a great deal of individual variation. In a spirit of amiable rivalry, each fraternity tried to top its neighbors. Zeta Psi did this with a colossal classical portico, a grandly theatrical gesture that required a theatrical architect. They found him in William Neil Smith, who was not only an architect of theater buildings (New York City's Nederlander Theater, 1921) but also a genuine eccentric who once designed a fourteen-story skyscraper for a golf club, several stories of which were to be set aside for playing golf in winter.

Smith suppressed his eccentricity to design an impeccably correct Ionic portico for Zeta Psi, today known as Wood House. It is the only one of the college's frat houses that would not look entirely out of place on the great Lawn of Thomas Jefferson's University of Virginia. But over time Smith's elegant Ionic capitals rotted, and in the late 1960s the college determined that it would be cheaper not to replace them but to turn them into the simpler Tuscan order. Unfortunately, the proportions of the rest of the classical order remain confusingly Ionic. Whatever students learn about classical architecture in the Art Department is instantly undermined the moment they cross Spring Street and encounter wayward Wood House.

81   Center for Developmental Economics (St. Anthony Hall)
McKim, Mead & White, 1884–85; Additions: architects unknown, 1905, 1927; PBDW Architects, 2017; Renovations: Centerline, 2017–18

A fraternity house leads a double life. Simultaneously a private house and a public building, it has to provide privacy and seclusion to its residents and open-handed hospitality to its visitors. St. Anthony Hall solves the problem with the simplest of means—rugged walls of rock-faced dolomite, a heavily battered tower, a ground-hugging roof—to make a private and cozy citadel. The architect swung that same roof out into space to make a broad and inviting porch so that the receptions within could spill out pleasantly into nature. It is an outstanding building—the work of one of the most brilliant architects ever to work at Williams College: Stanford White of McKim, Mead & White.

St. Anthony Hall is the affectionate name given to all the chapter houses of the Delta Psi fraternity. The Williams chapter was established in the 1850s, and one of its founding members was Frederick Ferris Thompson (Class of 1856), one of the most significant donors in the history of the college. He also was a generous supporter of St. Anthony Hall, and when it came time to build a chapter house in 1884, he provided an architect. White had just designed an opulent townhouse in New York for Thompson, who evidently felt that its graciously flowing plan and extravagant wainscoting would suit the fraternity.

St. Anthony Hall was clearly inspired by the college's newest building, Morgan Hall, and how it responded imaginatively to its location, both in its locally quarried dolomite and its whimsical gables pointing to the Dutch culture of the nearby Hudson Valley. White reprised those features, and his St. Anthony is a witty paraphrase of a Dutch Colonial house, compact in silhouette and terminating in proud stepped gables. But no Dutch house ever had such an audacious tower, tapered in the fashion of an Egyptian pylon. This was pure White, who had just used the form in his Lovely Lane Methodist Church in Baltimore (1883–84).

The interior is conceived as a trio of splendidly interlocking spaces: a squarish entrance lobby, a stair hall to the right generously paneled in bright oak, and beyond this a magnificently intimate living room. This space is the gem of the building, and the elaborate play of crossbeams on the ceiling combined with the heroically oversized fireplace are the rhetorical expression of those two most primal of needs: shelter and warmth. There is nothing quite like it on the Williams campus—it is as cozy as a Viking mead hall.

St. Anthony has been altered over the years, not always with sensitivity. A rear wing, added in 1905, burned down in 1926; it was rebuilt only to burn down again in 1927. Fortunately, the additions have been to the south, which has left its principal facade largely intact. Also intact is the memorial to Thompson, an exquisite bronze relief (1906) by the sculptor Augustus Saint-Gaudens. Williams

TOP **St. Anthony Hall, late 1880s**   BOTTOM **St. Anthony Hall with dining hall addition of 1926**

College did not acquire the building until 1972, the last of the fraternity houses to come to the college. Since then it has served as the Center for Developmental Economics, one of the college's two graduate programs.

By 2017, recognizing that the growing program needed more space, the college decided that the dormitory rooms should be converted to classrooms and a new residence hall be built. The conversion, which involves an extension to the rear and the re-creation of the missing cupola, was given to Centerline Architects, who had just completed Horn Hall. The new residence hall was given to PBDW Architects (Platt Byard Dovell White), who faced a complicated task: the new dormitory had to be hospitable to students from a wide variety of countries and climates, some of whose cultures required a separation of men and women. At the same time, it could not compete with St. Anthony but had to defer to it. Finally, the new dorm had to reduce energy consumption to the minimum. PBDW's solution was a low-slung two-story building that bent slightly in the middle to mark the entrance. This leads to a straightforward double-loaded corridor with pairs of bedrooms sharing a common bath (without windows, alas). The architects arranged the rooms artfully to house any possible combination of numbers of male and female students in separate wings.

Despite the obvious modern character, especially in the way the south-facing roof is angled to maximize its solar energy collection, the residence hall does not clash with St. Anthony. The authors of this book served on the architecture advisory committee that watched as the designs progressed, and noted how much thought the architects devoted to finding a color palette that complemented the gray stone and brown wood of the original building. In particular, various brick samples were studied on site under different lighting conditions. All was done with a perfectionist's zeal so as to respect White's masterpiece—and appropriately so, as one of the architects is a direct descendant of White himself.

82   Garfield House (Delta Upsilon)
New dormitory, SGA Architects, 2016–19

This broad property on South Street was the site of a modest house of 1851. In 1881 that house was replaced by a much larger Shingle Style structure with a tower, which became the retirement home of an alumnus. That house, in turn, was remodeled in 1924 into a half-timbered Stockbroker Tudor confection that became the home of Delta Upsilon fraternity. After the demise of fraternities, the college took possession of the property for student housing. As the building became increasingly expensive to heat and maintain, the college, despite a desire to preserve it, finally decided that a nineteenth-century, one-family house could not be remodeled to accommodate forty students comfortably while simultaneously meeting current building codes and the college's desire to decrease its carbon footprint. Demolished in 2018, the dormitory will be replaced by a new structure designed to respect the domestic scale of South Street.

83   Agard House (Delta Phi)
Architect unknown, 1900; Alterations, ca. 1927

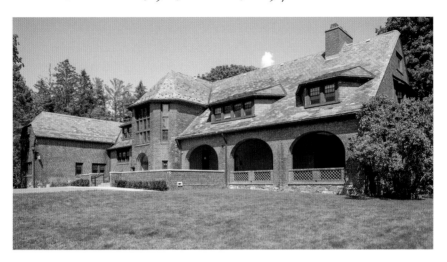

84   Fort Hoosac House (Phi Sigma Kappa)
Grosvenor S. Wright, 1931

85 Sterling and Francine Clark Art Institute

Daniel Deverell Perry, 1955; Manton Building: Pietro Belluschi and The Architects Collaborative, 1973; Cafe and Temporary Exhibition Galleries and Library Expansion, 2003: Ann Beha Associates; Lunder Center at Stone Hill: Tadao Ando, 2008; Additions: Tadao Ando, 2014; Remodeled Interiors of 1955 Building and 1973 Manton Building: Annabelle Seldorf, 2016

The Clark Art Institute is a fairly easy walk down South Street, but visitors who plan to spend time there may prefer to drive. While the Clark is very much an independent institution, its connections to Williams are close. The institute and the college jointly offer a graduate program in the history of art, and the majority of the Clark trustees are appointed by the trustees of the college. No visit to Williamstown is complete without a serious look at the Clark collection. Although the museum is famous for its holdings of French impressionist paintings, it contains many, many other treasures, such as first-rate examples of the art of Winslow Homer and one of the most important works of Italian Renaissance art in North America, Piero della Francesca's fifteenth-century *Virgin and Child Enthroned with Four Angels*. The special exhibitions every summer attract large crowds.

Robert Sterling Clark and his brother, Stephen Clark, were avid collectors of art, a pursuit made possible by a family fortune based on the Singer sewing machine. Had the brothers eventually combined their collections, it would have been one of the great repositories of French art of the second half of the nineteenth century. But they did not. Stephen Clark's collection went to the Metropolitan Museum of Art and the Yale University Art Gallery. Sterling Clark's came to South Street in Williamstown, to be housed in a white marble Greek temple. Here, in the southwest corner of the temple, Clark and his French wife, Francine, lived during their last years, and here, under its front steps, they now repose. Clark is often said to have declared, when asked to explain his choice of a little-known classical architect for his museum: "I don't want a goddam architect building, a goddam monument to himself."

Annabelle Seldorf has recently remodeled, with much success, the gallery spaces in the temple. The rather dreary original galleries have been treated to walls of deep, intense colors that show off the collection splendidly, although the lavender walls of the central, skylit court do not satisfy every visitor to that room, intended from the beginning to display the Clarks' collection of more than thirty paintings by Pierre-Auguste Renoir. Seldorf reconfigured the seemingly endless corridor along the north side of the building into intimate galleries that make fine

TOP **Clark Art Institute, 1955 building**   BOTTOM **Clark Art Institute, Manton Building**

paintings look even finer. The southern corridor, however, retains much of its original lack of character.

Subsequent additions have greatly enlarged the plan of the institute. To house and serve the graduate program in art history, the brutalist, granite-clad fortress to the south of the marble building was erected in the 1970s, under George Heard Hamilton, second director of the Clark and founding director of the graduate program. Pietro Belluschi furnished the design, which reflected the fortress mentality that many educational and artistic institutions had developed at a time of student rebellion. Inside the building is one of the best art history libraries in the country, open to the public on weekdays. Seldorf's recent renovation of the courtyard and ground floor, opened in 2016, has alleviated many of the shortcomings of the original building and, in particular, made the extensive collections of important prints, drawings, and photographs easily available to the public. This wing is now named the Manton Building in honor of generous gifts of endowment funds and British paintings by Sir Edmund A. G. Manton and his wife, Florence, Lady Manton. This building also contains an auditorium with first-rate acoustics for musical performances.

During the directorship of Michael Conforti, the world-famous Japanese architect Tadao Ando was hired to design a major addition of galleries for temporary exhibitions, as well as ample spaces for eating and shopping. To many admirers of Ando's work, however, this building is a disappointment. The addition, now the main entrance to the entire complex, lies behind and to the northwest of the marble original building. A seemingly endless wall of purplish granite, the same stone that clads the Manton Building, leads diagonally from the parking area down a long walk that finally arrives at a glass door and moves into an entrance hall. Immediately opposite that door is another that leads out onto a broad terrace overlooking artificial ponds and a manicured hillside. The visitor, brought into the building after a long, tiresome walk, is dumped instantly outside again. To the right of the entrance hall is a room, dubbed the Michael Conforti Pavilion, for which various new uses are constantly being found; to the left is the actual entrance to the museum complex. There one finds stairs and an elevator that lead down to the temporary exhibition galleries, which work very well, and the cafe. Both are underground. This is no problem for the galleries, which need no natural light, but it is dreadful for the cafe. The view while one eats is not of the glorious landscape into which the entrance hall thrust you but steeply upward to the feet of people walking on the terrace. Overflow for the cafeteria is in a white-walled room deprived even of that glimpse of the foot-fashion parade.

To gain the galleries in the original building, the visitor has to walk through the museum store (museums nowadays are businesses) and then down another long, diagonal walkway that leads finally to the permanent collection. Along the way one passes the names of donors, sized according to the amplitude of their donations—an embarrassing look at other people's checkbooks. The corridor ends in a glass-enclosed room that serves as the prelude to the galleries themselves. The light is bright, so one's eyes have to adjust abruptly to the dimly lit first gallery, where the superb collection of Homers forms the first exciting encounter with the museum's holdings. But there is no obvious place to go from this cul-de-sac. The experience is disorienting. You have actually entered into what once was the Clarks' kitchen, the back of the house. At the end of one's tour of the galleries, when one exits the dimly lit Homer gallery back into the brilliant light of the west-facing glass porch, the change can cause pain to the eyes.

Up Stone Hill from the Clark's main structures is a separate two-story, wood-clad structure, designed by Ando, that is reachable by a foot path or a winding paved road. The Lunder Center at Stone Hill houses the Williamstown Art Conservation Center on the bottom floor and additional galleries and a lecture hall on the upper level. The rectangular structure is pierced by a diagonal wall whose purpose becomes clear only when one walks out onto the terrace on the northwest corner of the upper level. Down below, the diagonal wall is cut open to reveal a wonderful Ando play with planes and solids and voids.

The upper, or southern, facade presents a Miesian, or even a Kahnian (as in the British Art Center at Yale), simplicity of structure and infill, punctured only by the entrance bay. This leads to an entrance hall from which one can choose galleries to the left, a lecture hall to the right, or a terrace in front. Here Ando's genius with relating architecture and landscape triumphs. Walk out onto the terrace and watch how Ando shifts the axis of movement diagonally to the right (thus the diagonal wall visible below), to bring the visitor face-to-face with the Dome, the mountain that dominates Williamstown from the north. For architecture lovers, this moment alone is worth the trip down South Street and maybe even the trip to Williamstown.

Clark Art Institute campus,
view from Stone Hill

ABOVE **Clark Art Institute, view of Lunder Center from the northeast**
OPPOSITE, TOP **Clark Art Institute, view of Lunder Center from the southwest**
OPPOSITE, BOTTOM **Clark Art Institute, terrace of Lunder Center**

86   Hopkins Memorial Forest

In the extreme northwest corner of Massachusetts, where the Commonwealth joins the states of New York and Vermont, is a parcel of land that is entirely typical of this region of low mountains and rapidly flowing streams. It is a landscape that shares a common history with most of the land between the Connecticut and Hudson Rivers. At the same time, the 2,500 acres, extending from the crest of the Taconic Range on the west to the Hoosic River on the east, that constitute the Amos Lawrence Hopkins Memorial Forest, have their own particular stories to tell and mysteries to unravel, making it a unique landscape as well. Before being settled by eighteenth-century colonists, it served the native Mahicans as a hunting ground. The European settlement of this land followed an uphill, centrifugal pattern in the second half of the eighteenth century, spreading westward from the fertile "marble valley" of the Hoosic toward the less-fertile, high-elevation soils of the Taconics.

At the regional peak in agriculture around 1830, the forests of this landscape were reduced to islands of woodlots, covering only 30 percent of land, "improved land" cleared of trees and roots and suitable for agriculture extending to the Taconic crests. Thereafter, agriculture literally went "downhill," as the small subsistence farms consolidated on the lower elevations with more fertile soils. After the Civil War further agricultural transformation occurred, as nearly all the hillside farms were abandoned, and Amos Lawrence Hopkins (Class of 1866), the sixth of Mark and Mary Hopkins's ten children, returned to Williamstown to establish the Buxton Farms. Between 1887 and 1910 Amos Hopkins amassed 1,636 acres in the northwest corner of Williamstown. His gentleman's farm became the "showplace" of agriculture in Williamstown, with a staff of dedicated local employees, including the young Arthur E. Rosenburg,

tending to the fields and livestock, even when the Hopkinses were at their Boston residence between October and April.

In 1912 Amos Hopkins died, and his widow, Maria-Theresa Burnham Dodge Hopkins, continued the Buxton Farms until 1924, when she auctioned off the livestock and most of the horse-drawn farm equipment, turning the responsibility for overseeing the property over to Rosenburg. Mrs. Hopkins attempted to liquidate the

property, but potential sales evaporated, especially during the early 1930s. In desperation, she offered President Harry Garfield the gift of Buxton Farms as a memorial to her late husband.

The gift was accepted, and through the efforts of Henry Lefavour, a Williams College trustee, the land was deeded for $1 to the US Forest Service to become the A. Lawrence Hopkins Experimental Forest in 1935. The land transfer was with the condition that should the Forest Service cease to use the land as a research forest, the title would revert back to the college. The initial research at the Hopkins Forest focused on timber management, facilitated through quarter-acre permanent plots in which every woody stem greater than a half inch in diameter was measured and counted, and its species recorded. Other forest data were also collected in this network of 220 plots that covered all the forested lands in this postagricultural landscape. The initial collection of data was made by the Civilian Conservation Corpsmen under the supervision of Norman E. Borlaug, who was taking a break from his forestry major at University of Minnesota to earn enough money for tuition for his senior year. In 1970 Borlaug would be awarded the Nobel Peace Prize for his later work in crop genetics and food production.

World War II led to the temporary closure of the Hopkins Forest, from 1942 to 1946. When research operations resumed, the Forest Service shifted emphasis from timber management to forest genetics. Rather than cut any trees down, it established plantations of hybrid poplars, ash, spruce, pine, larch, and other species in lands that Amos Lawrence Hopkins had used as pastures and hay meadows. These genetic plantations were monitored through the mid-1960s, when the Forest Service decided to vacate the property and return it to Williams College in 1968.

The college, for the second time in thirty-five years, had to decide what to do with this landscape. Some of the land abutting Bulkley Street and Northwest Hill Road was immediately converted into a housing development for faculty and staff or sold to private interests. In the autumn of 1970 Henry Art, a newly arrived faculty member in biology on the staff of the recently established Center for Environmental Studies, was tasked with creating a proposal for a field facility for environmental education and research. The report resulted in the creation of the Hopkins Memorial Forest, or actually the re-creation, and the purchases and gifts of additional adjacent lands, such as the Moon-Primmer Farm inholding and the old-growth woodlot that became known as the Beinecke Stand, increased its size to over 1,700 acres. Later acquisitions in Massachusetts, and adjacent New York and Vermont, have created a contiguous landscape of over 2,500 acres.

During the 1970s Professor Art and numerous students conducted a census of the permanent plots in the forest, extended the plot system to areas that had become forested since the 1930s, and obtained a grant from the National Science Foundation to renovate the carriage house, naming it the Rosenburg Center Field Station. The Hopkins Memorial Forest became a site for active student and faculty research, course field laboratory exercises, and passive recreation by members of the college and Williamstown community. Over the next several decades Professor David Dethier of the Geosciences Department, with the assistance of Jay Racela of the Center for Environmental Studies, renovated and expanded the weather- and stream-gauging stations, both contributing to the archive of meteorological data for Williamstown dating back to the early nineteenth century and providing an online presence for this information.

The Hopkins Memorial Forest has become a site for the study and monitoring of long-term changes in typical forested landscapes of western New England. The data relating to the site that have been collected are extraordinary and include a deed history dating back to the mid-eighteenth century; taxation, livestock, and land-use data dating back to the early nineteenth century; and quantitative data on vegetation, hydrology, meteorology, and other environmental factors dating to the early twentieth century. The "unmanaged woodlands" in the now-224 permanent plot system were censused in the 1930s, 1970s, 1990s, and 2010s—and will be monitored at roughly fifteen-year intervals. The Hopkins Forest also is a site for the study by students, faculty, and visiting researchers of contemporary environmental issues, such as invasive species, species interactions, changes in amphibian populations in vernal pools, and the impacts of global climate change on regional landscapes.

Hopkins Forest is reached by following US Route 7 north from Field Park, bearing left onto Bulkley Street, and turning right when Bulkley Street dead-ends at Northwest Hill Road.

by Henry W. Art, Rosenburg Professor of Environmental Studies and Biology

ENDNOTES

1 "Theta's New Lodge," *The Purple and Gold: Official Magazine of the Chi Psi Fraternity* 25 (1907–8): 196.

2 Ibid.

3 "DKE Plans Modern House at Williams. New Design Will Shatter Campus Tradition," *Berkshire Eagle*, June 13, 1959, 8.

4 "Recent Work by Squires and Wynkoop," *International Studio*, June 1909, cix.

5 Ibid.

6 "Notes and Comments: The Decorative Use of Brick," *Architectural Record*, September 1908, 9.

7 *Columbia Daily Spectator*, February 11, 1953.

Acknowledgments

Writing this book has been a labor of love—love for the Williams College campus and for its buildings. Both of us have spent most of our careers as architectural historians in the midst of it all. Despite the accumulated time on the faculty, now fifty-two (E. J. Johnson) plus twenty-four (Michael Lewis) years, we have learned more than we expected to learn about a place we thought we knew all too well. We have also come to realize that the stories we were told about many buildings, some quite amusing, were well-meaning "alternatives" to what actually happened. We hope that we have been able to straighten some of these out. The book has also been an extraordinarily happy collaboration between us, the two authors, and Ralph Lieberman, the photographer. All three of us are architectural historians who have been friends working together for many years. We have had a good time.

We are indebted to countless colleagues who have helped along the way. Three former presidents of Williams, John Chandler, Francis Oakley, and Morton Schapiro, have generously shared their recollections of their careers as patrons of Williams architecture, and Chandler was also able to take us back to the presidency of his predecessor, John E. Sawyer. And we are grateful to former president Adam Falk, who, together with former provost William Dudley, encouraged us to go ahead with this project. We also thank the current provost, Dukes Love, for his enthusiasm and support. Sheafe Satterthwaite critiqued the entire manuscript with a perspicacity that much improved many a page. Denise Buell, dean of faculty, and Nancy McIntire, retired assistant to the president for affirmative action and government relations, were both generous with much-appreciated help. Kenna Therrien of the Andover Historical Society revealed the existence of the house Edward Dorr Griffin built in that town.

Faculty and staff who have been involved in recent building projects—Amy Johns, Tiku Majumder, and Jason Moran—have provided firsthand knowledge based on their experiences. Wayne Hammond of the Chapin Library and the staff of the Williams College Archives, particularly Katie Nash, Jessika Drmacich, and Laura Zepka, have been unstintingly and eagerly helpful. Henry Art happily and generously supplied a splendid entry on Hopkins Forest. Charles Paquette in Visual Resources provided crucial and good-humored technical support. The Facilities staff under Rita Coppola-Wallace graciously gave us access to their collection of architectural drawings; Marsha Peters was wonderfully kind.

Over the years, our students have conducted independent research and made important discoveries that are incorporated in this manuscript; in particular, we thank Christopher Swan, Christopher Bell, and Josephine Warshauer. Finally, David C. Johnson gave help above and beyond the call of duty. We would like to thank the Williams security staff, in particular Nancy Macauley, for patience with many tiresome requests to unlock doors, and for sharing their remarkably wide knowledge of the campus and its curiosities.

Finally, we thank our wives, Leslie Johnson, Susan Glassman, and Valerie Krall, who have put up with far too much chatter about the buildings of Williams.

Brooks, R. R. R., ed. *Williamstown, the First Two Hundred Years, 1753–1953.* Williamstown, MA: McClelland Press, 1953. 2nd ed., *Williamstown: The First Two Hundred Years and Twenty Years Later.* Williamstown, MA: Williamstown Historical Commission, 1974. 3rd ed., *Williamstown, The First Two Hundred and Fifty Years 1753–2003.* Williamstown, MA: Williamstown House of Local History and Williamstown 250th Anniversary Committee, 2005.

Denison, J. H. *Mark Hopkins, A Biography.* New York: Charles Scribner's Sons, 1935.

Durfee, Calvin. *A History of Williams College.* Boston: A. Williams, 1860.

Griffin, Edward Dorr. *A Sermon Preached September 2, 1828, at the Dedication of the New Chapel Connected with Williams College, Massachusetts.* Williamstown, MA: Ridley Bannister, 1828.

Hopkins, Mark. *A Sermon, Preached at the Dedication of the New Chapel, Connected with Williams College. Sept. 22, 1859. By Mark Hopkins, D.D. President of the College.* Boston: T. R. Marvin & Son, 1859.

Lewis, R. Cragin, ed. *Williams, 1793–1993: A Pictorial History.* Williamstown, MA: Williams College Bicentennial Commission, 1993.

Malmstrom, R. E. *Lawrence Hall at Williams College.* Williamstown, MA: Williams College Museum of Art, 1979.

McElvein, Bruce Burr. "Williams College Architecture, 1790–1860." 2 vols. BA honors thesis, Williams College, 1979.

Perry, Arthur Latham. *Origins in Williamstown.* New York: Charles Scribner's Sons, 1894.

———. *Williamstown and Williams College.* New York: Charles Scribner's Sons, 1899.

Rudolph, Frederick. *Mark Hopkins and the Log: Williams College, 1836–1872.* New Haven, CT: Yale University Press, 1956.

———, ed. *Perspectives: A Williams Anthology.* Williamstown, MA: Williams College, 1983.

Spring, Leverett Wilson. *A History of Williams College.* Boston: Houghton Mifflin, 1917.

Stoddard, Whitney S. *Reflections on the Architecture of Williams College.* Williamstown, MA: Williams College, 2001.

Warren, Philip H., Jr. *What's in a Name: The Buildings of Williams College: A Collection of Essays.* Williamstown, MA: Williams College, 1999.

Image Credits

All photographs are by Ralph Lieberman unless otherwise noted.

American Architect and Building News (December 9, 1893): 74; Architectural Review (August 1905): 134t; Architecture (September 15, 1905): 33; Brickbuilder (February 1911): 36t, 198; Brown University, John Hay Library, University Archives and Manuscripts: 118; Library of Congress: 27, 29l, 71t, 219; Office of Facilities, Williams College: 42, 45t, 51, 67, 146, 156b, 184; Private collection: 71b; Purple and Gold, Official Magazine of the Chi Psi Fraternity (1907–8): 228; Royal Institute of British Architects: 23br; Sterling and Francine Clark Art Institute: 22m; Visual Resources, Art Department, Williams College: 177t, 234; Williams College Archives and Special Collections: 12, 17b, 19, 22t, 22b, 23tl, 23tr, 23bl, 25, 26, 27, 29r, 36b, 40, 44, 45b, 48, 66, 91l, 99, 113, 119, 132, 142r, 152, 158l, 165, 194, 211b, 220, 229t, 229m, 237t; Williams College Museum of Art: 15, 17t, 18, 21, 85, 124, 128

Index

Page references for illustrations appear in *italics*.